The CAT
Who Couldn't See
in the Dark

The CAT Who Couldn't See *in the* Dark

Veterinary Mysteries
and Advice on Feline Care
and Behavior

HOWARD PADWEE, D.V.M.
AND VALERIE MOOLMAN

CHAPTERS PUBLISHING LTD, SHELBURNE, VERMONT 05482

Published by
Chapters Publishing, Ltd.,
2085 Shelburne Road, Shelburne, VT 05482

Library of Congress Cataloging-in-Publication Data
Padwee, S. Howard.
    The cat who couldn't see in the dark: veterinary mysteries and
advice on feline care and behavior / Howard Padwee and Valerie
Moolman; illustrations by Barbara Smullen.
    p.   cm.
Includes index.
ISBN 1-57630-030-7 (hardcover)
1. Padwee, S. Howard. 2. Veterinarians—New York (State)—New
York—Biography. 3. Cats—New York (State)—New York—Biogra-
phy. 4. Cats—New York (State)—New York—Anecdotes. 5. Cats.
I. Moolman, Valerie. II. Title.
SF613.P24A3   1997
636.8—DC21   96-37630

Printed in U.S.A. by
R.R. Donnelley & Sons

Designed by Susan McClellan

Cover illustration by Bryan Leister

To my grandchildren,
Samantha, Alexander, Haley,
John and Charlotte
—S.H.P.

To Lyn,
For a helping hand that
must be about worn out by now,
my everlasting thanks.
—Val

Acknowledgments

WE JOIN IN OUR THANKS to Adrian Gerstel, for vignettes of backyard menageries; to the city of New York, for furnishing us with our outdoor office—Bryant Park behind the Public Library, where we taped cat stories and incidental bursts of midday music; to our agent, Jane Dystel, for putting us together with editor Rux Martin; to Rux, who makes work feel like, well, work, but working with her was a great pleasure; and to Zöe Lovell-Othen, the teenager who gave us Pawline's elegy.

Our thanks, too, to cats present—Teddy, Lulu and Floyd—and past: Honey, Flora, Clovis, Splotch, Wally Ballou, Darlin' Jill, Sweetie, Gracie, Waco, Buttercup and YumYum.

Howard Padwee's personal thanks: To my wife, Jane, for listening to hours of anecdotes.

Valerie Moolman's personal thanks: To my Park Slope neighborhood, with its concerned network of cat lovers, cat losers and, best of all, cat finders. (Lulu's ba-a-a-ck!)

Contents

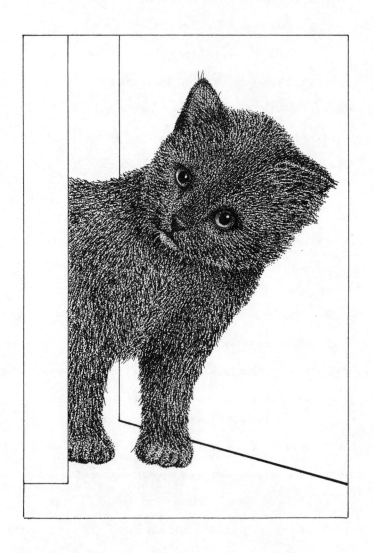

CHAPTER ONE

A Cat *in the* Night

LET ME PUT YOU IN THE PICTURE: It is a fall day some years back, and I am owner-operator and chief veterinarian of an animal clinic in a New York townhouse on Fifty-second Street near First Avenue on Manhattan's East Side. Around one corner of the block is a pharmacy, and around the other corner are brownstones and apartment houses. Catty-corner (no pun intended) across the avenue is Billy's, a landmark bar-restaurant justly famous for its steaks and chops.

My own place is something of a landmark, too. That is because of my flowers. My artificial flowers, I am sorry to say. "Oh, he's the vet with the plastic flowers! . . ." Well, they're not plastic, but they're not real.

Although my practice is firmly rooted in the city, I have moved myself and my budding family to more or less rural New York, where I have a sprawling old house snuggled among trees and cow pastures. My flower garden is my pride and pleasure, a blaze of color almost the whole year round. After a few seasons of country living, I found I could not bear to be without flowering plants throughout the long days in the city, and so I planted seasonal flowers in the tiny front yard and window boxes of my mid-Manhattan clinic.

Clients and passersby loved my flowers. They loved them so well that no new crop lasted for more than two or three days before admirers nipped them off for little bouquets or boutonnieres. Sometimes the perpetrators even wore them into my office. I suppose that says something about New York, but I'm not sure what. Anyway, I stood that for as long as I could—until my mini-gardens had been decimated for about the tenth time—and then one day, in an enormous huff, I ripped everything out. But I was not happy. The color was gone, and with it, the sense of somebody caring about enlivening an old brownstone. Something was missing. Something that was lovely and broke the gray monotony of life on Fifty-second and First.

I took my problem a few doors up the street to a neighboring entrepreneur. He was a supplier of stage props, specializing in theatrical floristry, and he cheerfully agreed to provide me with a change of flower arrangements every month for as long as I wanted them. He had a couple of dogs and a cat, so it was a done deal. He did my front garden; I did his animals.

There were people who didn't like my flowers, and a woman who lived in an apartment above Billy's said that they were "hideous," but for the most part they were a neighborhood triumph. I could see that they were a little on the stagey side, larger than life and twice as colorful, but I felt that was a distinct part of their charm. And they became an integral part of the East Side Animal Clinic. Also, nobody stole them.

Now then, this day is a day much like any other day.

I saw the kitten in the waiting room when I came out to look at my appointment pad and overheard those sneezing and wheezing sounds that invariably mean trouble. A young woman was holding a small black-and-orange cat in her arms and murmuring to it in the kitty baby talk that passes for client conversation in my practice. With her was a young man who acted like an anxious father hovering over an ailing child.

The little cat sneezed again. I noted that the eyes and nose were oozing and the whole tiny body was shivering as if in the grip of terminal hypothermia. Yet this was a mild September day.

As a rule I have my patients wait their turn, but I thought this small sneezer should be whisked into my consulting room right away before infecting anyone else with what appeared to be a respiratory virus. Nancy and John Gardner both came in with the patient. This in itself was unusual. It only takes one person to bring a two-to-three-month-old cat to a veterinarian. And normally, when an animal looks so miserable, the person uses a carrying case or at least a cardboard box. This couple had nothing but the cat. Yet they were not the street people who sometimes brought me strays. They were well-dressed and, I thought, responsible-looking.

I asked who had recommended them to our clinic, and they said they had been referred by friends who had a couple of dachshunds. As for themselves, they admitted, they had never brought an animal to a veterinarian before. In fact, they had never had an animal before. This one had just snuck into their tent one night while they were camping in the Catskills and simply attached itself to them. They had been captivated by it, so they took it home. That had been a few weeks ago. The truth of it was, neither of them knew anything about cats, but they just loved this kitty.

Now the cat was on the examining table, and it was shivering and shaking, an undersized kitten with scared eyes but still as irresistible as only a baby animal can be. I was making my own murmuring sounds, trying to get acquainted and settle it down. The cat tried to snuggle right into the young woman's coat and disappear. That was one good sign; it felt secure with her.

I ran my hands over its body and down over the tail.

"So it's never had any vaccinations," I commented. "No shots."

"Shots? What shots?" The couple looked taken aback. "Was he supposed to have shots? He looked perfectly healthy when we got him. Reason we came, he's just been through a bad experience, and now he's in terrible shape. Poor Tommy—it's all because we had to go away and leave him with that cat woman."

Poor Tommy? Still stroking, I lifted the scrawny tail.

"Tammy, maybe," I said. "Tommy, no. This is a female. See?" And I pointed out certain vital features of cat anatomy, specifically the female genitalia. This was like Biology 101, but the Gardners looked astounded at the wonders of nature.

"That? That's it?"

Well, I'm used to this; I can't tell you how many new cat owners have been similarly surprised. And the truth is, with the distinguishing parts on such a small scale, it's not always easy to determine the sex of a very young or undernourished cat.

"She's a nice little tortoiseshell tabby," I observed. "Torties are nearly always female. In fact, you can bet your last dime that a tortoiseshell is a female. Okay, so long as we're here, let's get her temperature."

We got a reading of 104. The normal temperature for a cat is 101.5 to 102; 104 would be consistent with a severe respiratory infection.

I removed the thermometer and checked out her coat.

As my thumbs cleared tiny pathways in the fur, I noticed minuscule black specks darting around in the soft fuzz of the underbelly and neck. Unlike the tiny genitals, these even smaller dots were absolutely unmistakable.

"Fleas," I noted. And a few moments later, "Ear mites."

There was a massive infestation of both of these nasty little parasites, very likely caught from another infected cat. Or perhaps she had brought them with her from the country. Most kittens have ear mite infections, especially those that come from pet shops, farms or any place where there are unsanitary conditions. Like a house with too many other animals in it.

"She been scratching her ears?"

Mrs. Gardner nodded. "Compulsively," she said.

"That usually means mites. But there don't seem to be any other visible abnormalities here." Nor any lumps anywhere on the skinny little body.

"How's her appetite?"

No appetite.

Well, she wouldn't have. She is obviously one sick kitty, and she may not even be able to swallow.

Now for those runny eyes and sneezes.

I checked the eyes and flushed out the pus-like discharge with a saline solution. She had a bad case of conjunctivitis, but the eyes were otherwise normal. I opened the mouth to check the teeth and throat and found that the kitty had severe laryngitis. No wonder I hadn't heard a meow.

Now for the heart and lungs. Congestion, I thought, was a probability. We had quite a set of symptoms here, and I was barely halfway through my basic examination.

Meanwhile, she was hungry and dehydrated and unable to swallow and the fleas were swarming briskly over her body.

I said: "Tell me again about picking her up in the Catskills. And that business of the cat woman."

And the whole sorry little tale came out. It started out cute: Nancy and John had gone camping for a few days that summer, pitching their tent in a wooded area bordering a farm. (Had there been wood ticks? I wondered. Maybe I had missed something. I searched. No, I didn't see any.) The farmer was a nice fellow; he had given his permission and sent them to the site with firewood and a loaf of his wife's freshly baked bread.

Very early one morning toward the end of their stay, a small furry presence made itself felt in their tent. Something started licking Nancy's face and leaving little whiskery tickles on her cheeks. After a few squeals of alarm, she realized it was a visiting cat, which she didn't especially appreciate because she simply was not an animal lover. Neither she nor John had ever had a pet of any kind. Besides, it purred too loudly, tried to cuddle up around her head, and started pulling at her hair. They chased it out; it came back; they chased it out; back it came. After a night of chasing, they saw, in the morning light, this adorable—their word—little kitten curled up on Nancy's sweatshirt.

Nancy touched it gingerly. It was very soft and strokable. John tickled it under the chin. Not knowing exactly what to do with the cat, they decided it must be hungry. They gave it some evaporated milk and a little canned tuna, and the cat gobbled it right up.

What to do with it?

They spent the rest of the morning playing with the cat and talking about it.

"Let's take it back to the farmer. It must be his."

"Let's take it back and ask him if we can keep it."

After consultation with the friendly farmer, whose top cat had recently produced a litter of six more-or-less similar babies, the Gardners had taken the kitten home and lavished affection on it. So far as they knew, all they had to do was give it cat food and cuddles and a litter pan. But after a couple of weeks they were called out of town on family business. Desperate to come up with some sort of cat-sitting or boarding arrangement for the alleged Tommy, they decided that there was nothing they could do but take the cat with them.

To take a barely broken-in kitten with you on a family emergency seems like the height of folly to me, but as it turned out, they did something totally different. Nancy had a stroke of luck, or something, when she went to the local supermarket the day before departure to pick up cat chow for the road and dinner for that night. Pausing at the meat counter, she observed an elderly woman buying fifteen pounds of gizzards.

What in the world, she wondered, would anyone want with fifteen pounds of gizzards?

"I'm going to cook this up in a big stew with rice," the woman was explaining to the butcher, "and feed it to my cats."

"You must have a lot of cats, lady," he said.

"Not a single one too many," she said, "and I love them all."

Well, Nancy got to talking with her, of course, and Mrs. McGonigle was happy to tell her the names and cute habits of some of her cats and explain how well she took care of them and occasional boarders as well.

Boarders! thought Nancy, an idea stirring.

But how many cats did the old lady have? Somehow Mrs. McGonigle managed to avoid answering, but fifteen pounds of gizzards could obviously feed a ton of cats.

And did Nancy have any of the little darlings herself? Only one? Oh, so Nancy had a problem about taking care of her new baby kitty? Just for a while? Not to worry; Mrs. McGonigle would happily board the cat for a modest fee.

Of course, the woman was a total stranger, but she lived not too far away in Nancy's neighborhood, and she could scarcely be interested in kidnapping an extra cat and holding him for ransom. A small deposit, the rest on pick up, what could go wrong?

And she really seemed like such a nice old lady. So knowledgeable about cats. So devoted to them. So concerned about their proper feeding, even cooking special meals for them. Why not? This was a heaven-sent opportunity.

A relieved and grateful Nancy put the cat in a cardboard box that afternoon and walked it around to Mrs. McGonigle's place a few blocks away. It was down on Henry Street, a rather more modest area than where the Gardners lived, but it was much the sort of place that Nancy had envisioned as the McGonigle home.

The old woman greeted Nancy and her shoe box with a welcoming smile and apologized for not asking her to come in. She had pots boiling on the stove, she said, and she was on the telephone, but she was ready to introduce little Tommy to the others. Nancy could hear some of those others meowing in the background. A little disappointed at not being invited in to see the place, she left the cat in the box with Mrs. McGonigle at the front door with a bagful of canned and boxed kitten food. Early in the evening, the Gardners flew to California to cope with the family crisis. It turned out to be more complicated than they anticipated, and Nancy had to call the house on Henry Street and tell the cat lady that they had been delayed. No problem, said Mrs. Mac. The cat was no trouble at all, and he was fine.

It was eighteen days before Nancy was able to pick up the cat, which Mrs. Mac had tucked into the same old shoe box—by now considerably tattered around the edges—and rush it back to her apartment. She opened the box: the lively little sprite she had left behind was sleepy, apathetic and sneezy. It didn't want to eat, it didn't want milk, its eyes were sticky with some kind of gunk and its hair stood out in stiff clumps. There also seemed to be things in its fur and ears, and it was scratching and shaking its head as if trying to get rid of something.

The Gardners, babes in the woods as they were, had no idea what to do. Finally, in desperation, they remembered that there were such things as animal doctors and called their friends the dachshund owners who told them about me. So here they were, having done absolutely everything wrong except come to my clinic.

By the time the examination and preliminary tests were completed, we had learned that the kitten had picked up a number of diseases and parasites from Mrs. McGonigle's cats, including severe conjunctivitis and an upper respiratory infection with congestion of the lungs. She also probably had roundworms, too, judging by the bulge of her tiny tummy, as well as a robust colony of fleas and an earful of mites. And there was a very strong possibility that she had pneumonitis, a nasty infection.

I couldn't help shaking my head. Just a few standard vaccinations would have prevented a lot of what was the matter with this little cat—including the pneumonitis, which reminded me of Mrs. Livingston. She was a well-educated, well-groomed, middle-aged woman who had brought a limp Persian cat into my clinic a couple of years before. Shah, a young fellow who was clearly well taken care of for the most part, had been listless for several days. He was sneezing, his nasal passages were completely blocked with discharge, his eyes were watering and his throat was painfully inflamed. I was pretty sure I knew what ailed him. A throat culture confirmed my diagnosis of pneumonitis.

"Mrs. Livingston," I said gently, "this is a very serious situation. You know, it could have been prevented with the proper vaccines.

Everything else being equal—including appropriate nutrition—all a cat needs to stay healthy is a regular program of vaccinations. I don't mean to preach, but Shah should have had his first shots when he was about six or eight weeks old."

"Doctor," she said, "I don't believe in medicating myself. I'm a Christian Scientist. I never go to doctors for myself. I'm here as a last resort because I'm afraid for Shah. I'm afraid he'll die without help. I don't think he shares my beliefs."

I didn't think he did either.

Nor did I like thinking of myself as a last resort, but I do believe that in Shah's case I was.

We pulled him around and gave him his vaccinations. Since then he's been coming in every six months for booster shots. He's a fine fellow of a cat.

Meanwhile, back to the Gardners. I liked them, but I had never met anyone quite so clueless about the care and treatment of cats. They seemed to think the kitten was a toy or something that came built-in with all the strengths and skills necessary for living with a couple who had a lot of love to give.

But love, I explained, was not enough. A cat is a living thing with particular needs, especially when it's only a baby. Warming to my theme, I gave them a two-minute rundown on basic kitten care and feeding, the value of preventive medicine, the vaccinations essential for all cats in these times of extremely contagious diseases, and stern warnings about strangers with huge households of cats undoubtedly exchanging infections.

"At this point," I said, "we're going to have to do some blood chemistry to be certain of what she does not have, as well as what she does. Then, when she's a little stronger, we'll vaccinate her against rabies, rhinotracheitis, feline leukemia, panleukopenia . . ." I stopped, because it was beginning to sound too much even to me. "It's all combined in only three shots," I added lamely. For amateurs in the cat care business, it was a lot to take in all at once.

The Gardners looked a trifle dazed, but they were attentive.

"First of all," I said, "we have to get rid of this colony of fleas and all the diseases they track around with them. But she's in no shape for a flea bath right now. She'll have to be sprayed. She also needs fluids immediately. In any event, this kitty is quite ill and should remain in the hospital for further tests and treatment. Yes, of course you can visit her. But first—it's spraytime for fleas."

I picked up the kitten and held her squirming little form inches from my face, looking into her gummy eyes. She hauled off and socked me on the cheek with a tiny paw. Sassy!

The fleas were running like tiny cattle at roundup time. I put the kitten down on the table again and maneuvered her little body around while I sprayed it with a mild flea insecticide—nothing too strong because of her weakened condition. As the spray touched her body, we could see fleas dying in droves. I combed them out of her hair and she looked around with interest, apparently feeling a little happier already.

"Okay, now for the fluids," I said. I asked the Gardners to wait for me in the examining room while I took the cat into our treatment room. I inserted a catheter into her jugular vein to get an IV solution of fluids and medication into her body—a sort of a cocktail to combat dehydration and pump in amino acids and vitamins for nutrition and antibiotics for the infection.

I watched her for a few minutes before leaving her with Chris, my assistant at that time, and although the drip was very slow, it seemed to me that—even as I watched—the little cat took on new life, like a parched plant drawing up water.

"I'll probably have to keep her here for a few days," I told the Gardners. "We'll do some blood work and other tests to determine specifically what else might be wrong with her. Unless of course—" and I fixed them with a very penetrating eye—"you decide you don't want to keep her after all. Because this is one really sick cat."

In the resultant uproar, I decided that they genuinely did want to keep her. For the time being, they left her with me.

It was no trick to determine that the cat had a very severe respiratory virus infection—the suspected pneumonitis—an infestation of round-worms, which happen to be communicable to people, and a galaxy of minor problems. She really was a specimen of almost everything that could be wrong with a cat at any one time, short of physical injury. But she was young and resilient, of sturdy farm stock. Astoundingly, she had perked up by about a thousand percent and was tugging at her catheter. We pulled it out; she ate and drank quite happily. I called the Gardners.

"As soon as she's completely recovered," I said when they came to re-trieve her, armed with a new cat carrier, "I'd like her to have those vaccinations I was telling you about. I promise you, she won't even feel them."

I picked her up to put her in her carrier, and once again, she whacked me on the face.

This was my introduction to a cat that came to be called Pawline be-cause of the perilous situations she had a genius for getting into.

Movie buffs of the early silents will recall the serial or chapter drama called *The Perils of Pauline*, the most famous of all serials starring the most famous of all serial queens—the one and only Pearl White, a trapeze artist who did her own stunts. Pauline's continuing saga was played as a series of hair-raising episodes with cliff-hanger endings. Typically, Pauline would be tied across the railroad tracks by the mus-tache-twirling villain (oncoming train approaches inexorably, toot-tooting silently) or trussed to the wing of a flying machine, which, pilotless, is spiraling toward earth. Fast fade! Pianola crescendo! At the beginning of the next episode, Dudley Do-Right or Hairbreadth Harry would appear—my Hero!—and scoop her up in time for her next disaster.

In the years to come, our Pawline would never meet an open clothes dryer she didn't like, nor an open oven door. If there was a radiator to be stuck behind, she got stuck behind it. If there was a squirrel in the backyard to have a fight with, she had to fight it. Open windows, open doors, open drawers, narrow spaces, mousetraps, philodendrons, heights and depths of various sorts—everything in life was a hazard to be investigated and challenged and surmounted. In the course of time, I came to know her very well, and not only Pawline, but many of the cats and other animals in her circle of acquaintances—all of whom have given me enormous pleasure and valuable instruction.

CHAPTER TWO

The Town
and Country Vet

I T PROBABLY ALL STARTED WITH THE BLUE-EYED CAT. I
have been a practicing veterinarian for over forty years, first
in New Jersey, where my practice ranged from small domestic
pets to cows and horses, and then in New York City, where it
included all the standard household pets plus parrots, macaws, lambs,
baby goats, lion cubs, pigs, mice, gerbils, chickens and iguanas, as
well as the occasional python and kinkajou. All this, and more, in the
heart of the city.

Deep down, I have always been a New Yorker. I was born in New
York City and moved to suburban New Jersey when I was too young
to have even noticed New York, but I have caught up since.

Why become a veterinarian, of all things?

I suppose it was inevitable.

During my growing-up years, we always had cats and dogs around the house. My mother was a big-hearted animal lover, a prize-winning horsewoman and collector of strays who could not keep her hands off any animal in need of affection and care. (She did draw the line at reptiles and creatures of moist or warty skin.) Something of her kinship with nature communicated itself to her children. There were four of us, two boys and two girls. My much-older brother Edward and I both became veterinarians. Our sisters chose more people-oriented professions.

So there I was in semi-rural New Jersey on the way home from school, looking down at this blue-eyed cat and wondering if I should pick it up. It was just sitting in the street, looking forlorn and skinny, so dirty that I could scarcely tell that it was white. I bent down to pet it, and it reached up to touch me with its paws. Even as a scruffy, un-sentimental eight-year-old, I couldn't resist. I picked up this pitiful little thing, put it in my jacket and took it home. My mother wouldn't mind, I thought. It wasn't like the toad I had brought home the week before.

My mother cooed and clucked over it. We had one cat at the time, an ancient we called Aunt Agnes, who was secure in her knowledge that the house and everything in it was hers. She was above trivial questions of territory. She let us live in the house, she let the German Shepherd, Prince, live in the yard, and another inferior creature around the place wouldn't make any difference to the venerable Aunt.

True to herself, Aunt Agnes paid no attention when my mother borrowed some of her cat food for the guest and put it on the floor with a bowl of milk—but not in Agnes's dining area, because that would have been stretching tolerance too far. The little cat ate as if it had never eaten before, but of course they usually do that. Afterwards it started washing itself and purring like a coffee grinder. Then it forgot what it was doing and stopped washing in mid-lick, one leg still in the air.

"That's ridiculous," said my mother to the cat. "You'll never get clean that way." And she scooped it up and headed for the bathroom.

"No doubt it's riddled with fleas, too," she said briskly, lining the basin with a hand towel and turning it into a miniature bathtub.

Together, we held the squirming cat to keep the water out of its eyes and soaped the rest of it into a fine lather until the water turned gray. Then we rinsed, taking care around the face and ears, and towel-dried until a fluffy kitten emerged—sparkling white, beautiful, and a boy.

We wrapped him in a warm, dry towel, and I sat down with him on my lap. Once again he began to purr. He gave me little licks on my hands and butted me with his tiny head. I was captivated.

My thought in bringing him home was not so much to move him in with Agnes but to rescue him from the streets and feed him up. Then we'd try to find out if anyone was missing a cat of his description, and I would be the hero who had found him. Or else we'd have to take him to an animal shelter. We'd had transients before and always managed to place them.

"Hey, Mom! Let's keep him. We'll call him . . ."

"Don't give him any names yet," my mother said. "Let's see if anyone claims him first."

We put the word out. For days we asked around, but no one seemed to know anything about a missing kitten. So he became our pet. My first full-time cat. Aunt Agnes didn't count. She was more than twice my age, and I always thought of her as some sort of maiden aunt not meant for kids to play with . . . not like Snowman, first name Frosty, pure white except for his blue eyes.

We found Frosty the Snowman to be almost everything a kitten should be—lovable, docile, playful and cuddly. He did make little running attacks on Agnes and occasionally on the furniture—Agnes twitched and batted him away, the furniture suffered mildly—but this was part of his charm. What did strike us as not quite standard cat behavior was his obliviousness to sound. He never responded when we called him. If the doorbell rang, he didn't react; he didn't run to the door or away from it. Now our doorbell wasn't one of those low-pitched ding-dong chimers. It screeched like the fire drill alarm at school and would jerk you out of your chair if you were quietly doing your homework. If you slammed a door shut with a bang or dropped a heavy object on the floor, he didn't turn a whisker. He didn't even answer to the dinner bell or the can opener, which was remarkable. In the beginning, I thought it was some form of animal insolence, but my mother felt that Frosty was probably deaf.

When the cat was about three months old, we took him to a veterinarian for a series of standard shots and found out that my mother was right, as usual. We explained the hearing situation, and before even examining the ears and hearing structure, the vet said, "He isn't disobedient, he's deaf. He just can't hear." And this, he explained, was because of a genetic glitch in cats with white coats and blue irises. Many blue-eyed cats, he said, were congenitally deaf. I found this fascinating.

Chance and a youthful bent for entrepreneurship led me to meet most of the cats in my suburban neighborhood when I was about ten years old. My venture started when a neighbor who happened to have several pets asked me if I would go to the local market and pick up groceries for her. I did that, many times, noting that she always had a large order of cat food. Then another neighbor asked me if I would do the same thing for her, and I observed that she, too, was getting cat food in her order. That gave me the idea for a little bit of private enterprise: I would go into the cat food business. So I started buying cat food by the case, loading it onto my Flexible Flyer wagon and hawking it around the neighborhood at a slightly inflated price per can. Word got around that I'd established a pet food route, and pretty soon I had quite a list of customers who were willing to pay a few pennies for my delivery service. I even had some cards printed up to solicit extra trade. Running the business and making a little money was fun, but there was another reward: I got to know and play with all the pets in the neighborhood.

By the time I was fourteen, my brother Edward was a vet with a flourishing practice and I was already seriously interested in veterinary science. I think the moment of truth came for me when my brother was doing a cesarean on a mama cat, attended by an elderly anesthetist operating the old-fashioned ether machine that was then the state of the art. I happened to be along at the time because it was an emergency operation with complications and my brother had suggested that I come and watch. A cat breeder had called him at home after hours and said that one of his queens was having difficulty giving birth. Could he bring her right over to the clinic?

He could. We met there, and Edward sent him home to wait.

The cat was in real trouble. The first kitten in the birth canal was turned sideways, and there was no way the kittens could be delivered normally. It would have to be a cesarean. My brother and his aged assistant, Gerard, a highly qualified and experienced anesthetist, prepared the cat for surgery.

This was many years ago, when ether was considered the safest anesthesia. Gerard's task was to hold the ether cone over the cat's nose and administer the ether. This he did, and the operation proceeded.

I thought at one point that I was catching a faint whiff of ether in the air, but—what did I know? I certainly didn't know that Gerard wasn't feeling any too well that day.

Busy pulling out the kittens, my brother noticed too late that his assistant was leaning farther and farther over the operating table, gradually inhaling the cat's ether until he had one blast too many and crumpled to the floor. For a moment, Edward was too perplexed to do anything but stare, not knowing which situation to handle first—the cat, the ether or Gerard. We decided against Gerard and let him lie there while Edward finished the surgery, and I leapt to the task when he called on me to take over for the snoozing assistant. As soon as he was done, we moved Gerard to a couch by an open window and let him rest more comfortably.

The operation was a success. Mother and all five of her kittens were fine. The anesthetist woke up after a while and said he had not been feeling well but now he felt just great.

That experience was my inspiration. There was no turning back.

After high school in New Jersey, I worked on a farm, a prerequisite for veterinary school. When decision time came, I chose to go to Michigan State University, which had then and still has a fine veterinary school, and to me it made sense to do my practical pre-college training in middle America.

Going to veterinary school clearly offered a lot of advantages to a kid who loved animals. In this case, one advantage was the opportunity to exercise the horses at the veterinary school. There was one horse more special than the others: He was a blood donor, kept at the hospital as a pet between donations. He required a lot of exercise to keep in trim. I was able to ride him on the campus bridle paths daily. And there were others that also needed to stretch their muscles and run. I wound up getting free rides all over campus.

During summer and other vacations, I worked with various veterinarians for experience, plus room and board and a little spending money. Summer was a breeze, but winters were rough. One Christmas vacation job was in Michigan, with a father and son veterinary team. They had a big family, and instead of boarding with them, I lived in a neighboring house. Their routine was to pick me up at five-thirty A.M. to start our rounds together through snow that was four feet deep. It was pitch dark at that horrible hour, and very, very cold. They would honk the horn, and I'd tear down the stairs and leap into their car.

First stop each morning was the local slaughterhouse, where, as the law decreed, it was our duty as veterinarians to inspect all the food animals that had been slaughtered or were about to be. So far as I was concerned, it was not the greatest way to start a day, but before we began, we ate a convivial breakfast in the little employee restaurant attached to the slaughterhouse. It was a small but cozy place, just big enough to hold three or four tables, warmed by a potbellied stove and a big kitchen range topped with sizzling pans. Every time I was there, I sighed with contentment and thought what a perfect place this was to

be on a cold winter's morning. The food, too, was perfect, and plenti-
ful: eggs, bacon, sausage—we knew it was fresh—home fries, chunky
pieces of toast and relays of fresh coffee.

The dining room cats, primarily hired as mousers, looked forward
to our visits and became very friendly. One little black-and-white kitten attached itself to me, quite possibly because I gave her a piece of bacon each morning, and after a few mornings, it became accepted that
she was My Cat. On my last day, the owner officially gave the cat to me.

I took her back with me to Michigan State to start the next semes-
ter, only to find out that no cats were allowed in the dorms. So I made
arrangements with the caretaker of the veterinary school to board Nelly
there, and for the next four years, she was partly my cat and partly the
vet school's official resident cat. After graduation, I took Nelly home
with me to my mother's house, where she became a Padwee Domestic
Shorthair, a family pet for many years thereafter.

Another job I had was with a veterinarian out in Nebraska. I'd never
been to Nebraska before. When I got there, my new employer showed
me to a small room above the veterinary hospital, my home for the
weeks to come. Luckily for me, he also had a couple of mousers roam-
ing around the hospital, which took the edge off my solitary state.
One of the cats became attached to me and used to stay up in my
room as my companion.

This was a mixed practice that consisted mostly of small animals—
dogs and cats and pigs—but also some cattle. On one of my first days
there, we had a case of a beef cow giving birth to a calf. I had had experience with birthing cows before, but they had been milk cows. So
when the vet asked me if I had had any experience, I naturally told
him I did. "Fine," he said, "we'll see if you can deliver the calf."

Right. No problem.

I pretty soon learned that there *was* something of a problem. By
this time I had become accustomed to Michigan cows. And Michigan
cows are gentle. In a very great hurry, I learned that the ones out in
Nebraska are completely different. Soon as I got near her backside,

her two hind legs flew out at me and I was looking at hooves in the face. I leapt out of the way with only a breeze to spare. Like a bull in a ring, she turned and lunged at me. Luckily, I was not only very fast but very determined. This cow wasn't going to get the better of me, least of all when my boss was watching. Next round, she landed a light one on my chin, but I was getting better at this. With the coolness of long practice—which I hadn't had—and a little help, I got the restraints on her. She struggled briefly, then subsided. No big deal, I said to myself, hoping I looked nonchalant, and talking softly to the mother, I delivered the calf.

After graduation, I took a job with an elderly veterinarian in northern New Jersey. Half of his practice consisted of farm animals, mostly large, such as cows and horses, pigs and sheep; and the other half of dogs, cats and other household pets. He had a small animal hospital behind his house and a kennel where he boarded dogs. I got a lot of good experience working for him and his varied clientele—pigs to cats to dogs to sheep to horses and cows in no particular order, and no chance to get bored.

After about four months he made me responsible for all the night calls, which meant country driving late at night, in snow, rain, sleet or hail—it never seemed to be nice weather—spending maybe thirty, forty minutes driving to a farm and maybe ten minutes in the barn taking care of the animals.

There were lots of emergency calls both day and night, but most of them came during my late-night eleven P.M. to three A.M. shift. Getting called out in the middle of the night, often in the darkest hours before dawn, became almost an expected ritual. But not all the calls were totally routine. I remember one I got on an absolutely black, moonless night, from a farmer named Joe Richie, who had milk cows, sheep, a couple of horses, countless chickens, two dogs and apparently a house cat I hadn't known about. Usually, according to my senior partner, he was a phlegmatic, cheerful character who even managed to have most of his emergencies in broad daylight. But I had never met him, and my first impression of him on the telephone that night was of a man who was as nearly hysterical as any man I'd ever heard. His cat was about to give birth, he said, and she was in terrible pain. Would I please come out right away?

Well, sure I would. But I was a little puzzled. I hadn't even known he had a cat, and couldn't figure why he should be so frantic about it. It's not as if it were a cow. . . . Maybe it *was* a calf. No, he'd definitely said cat. Maybe it was some exotic breed, prize-winning Princess Purrina of—of what? Pelham? Princeton? Newark? My imagination got stuck there.

I drove for miles until I finally saw the dim outlines of what appeared to be his barns and then took a curve and saw the Richie house giving off a blaze of light. Joe Richie met me at the front door, and we went into the house together. He gave me a rather bleak look. "You're not her usual doctor," he said. "Well, no," said I, introducing myself. "I'm on night duty."

He nodded. "We'll go upstairs. Hurry, please."

We went upstairs and he motioned me into a bedroom. A woman was lying in a huge double bed, moaning.

"I don't understand," I said stupidly. "Where's the cat?"

"Cat? What cat? My wife's in agony, the baby isn't coming right, and you ask me about a *cat?*"

"Sir, I'm sorry, but you called a veterinarian, and here I am. I'll do anything I can to help, but I think we'd better get a human doctor, I mean your wife's doctor, or an ambulance, as soon as possible."

"Oh, what a fool I am," he groaned. "Oh Katya, Katya . . ."

Katya?

"Sir, who is your medical doctor? Your personal physician?"

I got on the phone, woke up the family doctor, sent for an ambulance, sent Joe down to the kitchen to boil water because that's what I'd heard you always do for farmers' wives unexpectedly giving birth, and sat down beside Katya to deliver a few soothing words and possibly—I prayed not, not me—a baby.

Help arrived. The baby came later. I was unspeakably relieved.

Possibly it was a decisive episode in my career as a country doctor.

It helped me realize that I wasn't doing what I'd thought I'd be doing as a veterinarian. I enjoyed taking care of farm animals, and even the occasional human, but the awkward hours and endless night driving were getting to be too much. It was making less and less sense to drive for hours over all kinds of rough roads in all kinds of dreadful weather to spend perhaps five minutes in a barn. My back was beginning to hurt me, and I was too young for that. More important, it was impossible to do comprehensive work on large animals in the unsterile conditions of country practice. What was much more satisfying was the intricate, far-reaching orthopedic and other surgery I could do in the clean operating room of a small-animal hospital.

I liked working with small animals. I wanted to. And so I decided to look for another position, preferably a more civilized practice in the city. Which is why I wound up in Manhattan, where I eventually bought the brownstone on East Fifty-Second Street and hung out my sign.

The practice grew rapidly, and soon we expanded to two brownstones side by side. One was designated for cats and the other for dogs. This is not to say that they each had whole buildings to themselves, because in fact the patients were as varied as the clients, and on any given day, I might be seeing not only cats and dogs but a whole range of creatures from pythons to monkeys and birds to rats. But I did like to board the cats and dogs separately, except for intensive care and recovery. I did this specifically because I wanted the cats to feel content while they were in the hospital, and a barking dog could upset them.

It also became necessary to enlarge my staff. At any one time I might have ten or twelve or even fifteen people working for me. The clinic had two receptionists, one secretarial and one to receive clients, and occasionally a third when needed. We had a bookkeeper who recorded billing information, which in recent years has been handled by a computerized billing service. Two associate doctors reported to me; two technicians administered medications, prepped the animals for surgery, watched their fluids, and generally kept an eye on the patients. An extra technician did night duty, and a tech was always on duty in the recovery room. Depending on animal occupancy at any given time, we had three or four kennel men to bathe and feed our guests, and we had a groomer to take care of coats and manicures.

The diversity of the practice was fun for me, but as time went by, I had another realization: *Cats* were the most fun. I was enchanted by their sheer entertainment value, the range of their personalities and the love they elicited from supposedly stony-hearted New Yorkers. In time it became one of my favorite tasks to unravel the puzzles brought to me by cat people: How can he eat so much and still lose weight? Why does she bump into the furniture at night? Why are his teeth rattling around loose in his head? Why can't she hear when I call her?

And so I became an insatiable cat detective and solver of feline medical mysteries, involving not so much Whodunit? as Whatisit? Whyisit? and WhatdoIdonow?

CHAPTER THREE

The Trouble *with* Strays

FUNNY THING ABOUT DOGS AND CATS: Most dogs are acquired by people who have decided to get one and pretty much know what breed of pup they want. Then they go out and get it. Cats, as often as not, just happen to people. They appear, like Pawline, and next thing you know, they have insinuated themselves into your home and your heart. They hop into open car windows at supermarket parking lots. They spring over fences into yards they like better than their own. They show up, unasked, on doorsteps. Or someone brings a basketful of unplanned kittens to the local greenmarket—or maybe flea market would be more appropriate—and plays cute with them until sympathetic fellow citizens decide they're too adorable to resist. Think twice! Because they are irresistible, and that's the trouble with cats.

In my own experience, cats are always attaching themselves to me, and I must admit I am a pushover. Almost every cat I've ever owned has just kind of shown up and adopted me, possibly because I tend to feed them little tidbits from the table. But I've never yet had the experience of a full-grown cat literally hammering at my back door and begging to be let in.

That was the case, long ago, with Patch, who clearly knew he had to find a home and family of his own. None of the humans realized he was slowly dying, but I think somehow he did.

I met Patch and his adoptive family through Pawline. She had settled happily into the Gardner home, an elderly low-rise city apartment house. Down the street from the Gardners' place was a row house in which their friends the Lombardis lived. Frank and Edda were both writers who worked at home much of the time. When not working, they often sat outside in their tiny backyard, a little postage stamp of an area reached through their basement door. There they would put out a couple of chairs and read, and pretend they were doing research.

These were people who had always known cats and loved them well. Before I entered the picture, they had in their household two aging Siamese cats about fifteen, maybe sixteen, years old. A few years before, they had had to part with a female tabby named Sugar, a rather haughty cat with a gastrointestinal problem who existed with the others in a state of mutual disdain, and the Lombardis had kept toying with the idea of getting another animal. But Buster and Daisy, they were sure, would not take kindly to the idea. There just did not seem to be any chemistry between the geriatric Siamese siblings and any other animals.

Buster and Daisy, I was told, had grown up entwined with each other. They slept in each other's arms in a heart shape that made them seem one eternally loving couple. But regularly, once a day, Buster started a fight. He would emerge from a sound sleep, back away from Daisy and give her one mighty whack on the head. She would whimper and hiss and run away with Buster in hot pursuit. Edda thought this was disgraceful. When the female cat had first come to her, she said, she had been a fine, upstanding career girl, showing every sign of growing into a high-powered woman executive. But when Buster had moved in a few months later and thrown his weight around, she had turned into a helpless female, browbeaten and whimpering, and they had established what became a lifelong pattern of cuddles and clouts and more cuddles. It was not hard to see why an extra animal might feel out of place.

All this was told to me by the Lombardis when they first came to my clinic with a lovable stray. What it meant to me, and what the rest of their story confirmed, was that they were genuine cat lovers who took both loving and intelligent care of their pets—so far as they knew.

What happened was this:

One day when Frank was outside reading in the yard, a rangy, rather dirty but sleek-coated white cat with a black half-mask and a couple of black body patches came cautiously over the fence and slowly edged up to him in the magical way that cats do: sitting quietly when watched, moving silently when not, two paces closer and sitting in po-faced silence when observed . . . walking and freezing, watching and waiting . . . walking and freezing . . . until he was at Frank's knee and butting his head against the man's leg for some energetic stroking. Frank obliged. The cat wanted more.

This was nice, but Frank wasn't truly interested in the cat's advances and after a while tried to shoo him away. The cat moved back a few feet but stayed in the yard. He was skinny, Frank noted, so his affection probably came from being hungry. Yet he seemed to be well-kept and domesticated, except that he had no ID tag.

Next day, same thing, except this time Frank went inside and brought out a can of cat food. The cat ate with interest but without any show of ravenous appetite. Then he came over to rub his head against his benefactor. "Sit down, now," said Frank. "Sit, sit." He gently pushed the cat down, and it stretched out at his feet. Frank thought to himself, "Looks like ink blots on his coat. Or splashes of black paint. Patches, actually. Kind of funny looking. But a sweet face. A nice fellow."

The cat's pattern of behavior was repeated with minor variations for the next several days. Always, he would come over to stroke and be stroked, and then lie down and purr. There was, of course, neither collar nor tag, but Patch—now he had a name, and that is a defining point of a relationship—acted as though he had grown up with affectionate people but had somehow lost them. He seemed to want love as much as he wanted food.

Then the pattern changed.

He started to appear on the fire escape at odd hours, looking in through the bedroom windows. For two or three days, not necessarily consecutive, he darted from the yard into the basement and stayed there until Frank found him hiding behind some boxes and took him back outside. By this time, Edda had also met him several times. Both she and Frank were getting quite fond of him. He was not a terribly handsome cat, but there was something very appealing about him— not just his rather odd looks but something curiously deferential and at the same time desperate. He *wanted* them. He wanted to be with Frank and Edda; he wanted to be in their home.

So they decided to invite him in. Now he turned skittish and elusive. He avoided the yard for a day or two and sometimes sat on the fence, just looking. Then he started climbing up and down the fire escape. One day, on the fire escape landing, he paced back and forth outside the partly open bedroom window.

"Okay, this is our chance," said Frank, quietly raising the window while Edda cooed at the cat and stood by with a towel to wrap around him in case he got nervous about coming in.

He just stood looking at them from the fire escape, not moving.

Frank reached out to the cat and took him in his outstretched arms.

Suddenly he had an armful of a whirling dervish of a cat, an agitated bundle of flying, flailing legs trying to make a getaway. "Quick! The towel!"

Well, Edda got the towel around the cat and rocked him in her arms.

What was really quite remarkable was that he hadn't hissed, he hadn't scratched, he hadn't bared a fang. He'd just gotten a little nervous there for a minute.

He went under the bed for about an hour and then came out to explore the apartment. Daisy and Buster were perturbed by his arrival and backed away with low growls. He observed them in silence and kept his distance.

Days passed. The cat now answered when he heard the name Patch. The Lombardis fed him, combed him, poured out their affection. When he seemed settled, Edda carried him around, in a basket, to the nearest vet, who happened to be about two blocks away. The vet gave him the standard shots and a flea shampoo, and Edda walked him back home again. From an ordinary, rather funny looking cat, he was now transformed into an absolutely dazzling creature with a full and almost flowing coat, soft as silk and glinting like snow with a few coal-black patches in it. He was a sweetheart of a guest with only one flaw: he sprayed. He was a territorial male. He sprayed at doors, on thresholds and on carpets; he shot a stream at Frank's trousers, and he backed up against Edda's bare leg and landed a zinger. Splat!

"Eeeyucch!" said Edda. "Aarggh! Beast! Yuck!"

The splatting of Edda precipitated another visit to the nearby veterinarian, who said that he was about one and a half years old and that he would have to be neutered if he was to be a longtime companion. The vet did the necessary, and the walk-in went home again with the Lombardis.

He stayed with them and filled out nicely. Edda found him to be a particularly sweet and cuddly cat, an affectionate armful who loved to stretch out alongside a napping person on a somnolent Sunday: a living teddy bear with a resonant purr. Daisy and Buster were still less than thrilled, but they allowed him to share their big water bowl and kitty potty. Patch was as serene as Santa Claus. He never raised a paw, never gave a hiss or a growl. And his new people loved him as if they had always been a family. It seemed to them that he truly loved them in return.

Do cats love? It is an eternal question among animal lovers. I think, in this respect, they are much like people. Some do; some don't; some love more than others; some don't know how, because they have not experienced love. Patch had known love at some time, and now he was experiencing it again.

A few months later, Daisy started fading visibly. She was up in years, so it was no great surprise, but her downhill slide was unexpectedly rapid. She lost her appetite, she staggered when she walked, and her teeth rattled loosely in her head. Well . . . so this was old age, the Lombardis said to each other. And if that's what it was, it was awful. After days, even weeks, of soul-searching, Frank and Edda made a final appointment for Daisy with the veterinarian who had regularly treated the Siamese siblings.

Dr. Sam looked into Daisy's eyes, gave her a sedative and put her into Edda's arms. A few minutes later, when she was purring very tiredly and softly, he slipped her a final, painless shot. It was very simple, very easy. Frank and Edda both cried.

Perhaps three months later, Buster began to wobble when he walked. His eyes were cloudy, he was salivating heavily, and his old combative spirit was gone. Soon, he too was gone, thanks to the gentle ministrations of Dr. Sam.

But what had been wrong with them?

Their symptoms were confusing and difficult to pin down. There seemed to be no definitive cause for them. Perhaps because the cats were old, their immune systems were down, and all systems had failed. It was sad.

The big cat who had come in from the cold was thriving. He was cuddly and contented and minded hardly at all when the Lombardis came back from a country weekend bringing with them a little ball of marmalade fluff called Tiger, a six-week-old orange male tabby who was endlessly playful and captivating.

Edda, in particular, was enchanted with his perfect little body, small enough to fit into the palm of her hand, his alert golden eyes, the way he explored every crevice and surface in the house, the way he chased his tiny little tail and laughed—she said—while doing it.

I thought that might have been stretching it a bit, but I myself have seen cats enjoying themselves so much I could have sworn they were laughing.

The little guy loved Patch. He followed him all over the house, pounced on him from around corners and jumped onto his back from chairs and windowsills to hitch free rides and tease him. Patch regarded all this tolerantly, like an elder statesman or a benevolent uncle. The only time he got a little tense was when Tiger leapt onto his back, as if he were a circus pony, and clung on with his tiny sharp claws. That, Patch seemed to think, was an undignified situation for the top cat in the house, and he took to speeding up when he saw Tiger lurking overhead. The little cat didn't mind. He played with his toys. Edda tied a fuzzy toy to a stair rail on an elastic string, and Tiger leapt at it and batted it around with endless enjoyment. He crawled inside slippers, played tag with woolen balls, chased imaginary mice—Edda said they were imaginary—and ran circles around Patch. Sometimes he just sat down in front of the big cat and peered up into his face, ready to play or skitter away across the living room, daring the big fellow to follow.

All in all, they got along splendidly, the joyous little fellow and the mellow one.

But then Patch started tiring of the games. His appetite flagged, and he became increasingly subdued. His big black eyes became cloudy and started to bulge, and his mouth filled with saliva. The Lombardis took him to their vet.

Patch was too young to be suffering from old age. Yet his symptoms were ominously familiar.

Dr. Sam checked him out, looked grave, took a blood sample. A few days later the results came back: feline leukemia virus.

It was not very well known back then, but it was thought to be incurable, irreversible, unstoppable. If Patch had it, he was mortally ill. He might live for two or three months, or he might, with care and treatment of his symptoms, hang on for a year or more.

Now it seemed that he must have brought the virus into the household and passed it on to Daisy and Buster. Being much older cats, they would have been susceptible to this extremely contagious disease. The virus is not communicable to humans, but it's deadly for cats. In a multicat household, it passes from one to another through bodily fluids and excretions, spread from the affected cat through common use of food and water bowls and litter pans. Grooming, licking, sneezing and anything else that transfers saliva would also do it. If there were any other cats left in the household, they were at risk, if not already affected.

The Lombardis agonized. They could not bring themselves to part too soon with the adoring stray, top cat in the household, and they didn't want to lose baby Tiger.

Their friends the Gardners suggested that they get a second opinion and another test. They brought Patch to me.

It was instantly evident that he was quite a sick cat. His eyes were half-closed, saliva literally poured out of his mouth, and according to Edda, his energy level was at a low ebb. And yet he was his gentle, affectionate self: still stroking and soliciting strokes; still eating, though less; still playing with Tiger, though less; still wanting to be with his people, and staying even closer to them than before.

We did a second test. It came back positive for FeLV—the dreaded feline leukemia virus.

FeLV is a terrible and complex disease that blocks the cat's natural ability to fight off other diseases. In effect, it attacks the immune system. Cancer of the lymph system, anemia, severe and progressive infection of the gums, infections of the bladder, kidneys and upper respiratory tract, infectious peritonitis—any or all and more of these could attack the infected cat. And there is no cure, not even yet. But some of the symptoms may be treated with antibiotics or chemotherapy or blood transfusions, and the cat might even go into remission for a period of time.

"That's what we're going to have to do," I said. "Treat his symptoms. At this stage, I'd suggest vitamins and minerals to bolster his energy and an antibiotic against secondary infections. I don't think any more heroic measures would be helpful." I picked him up. He looked at me with trusting eyes.

"Take him home now," I said carefully, wondering if this was indeed the wise thing to do, "and don't let the little kitty get near him. Keep them completely isolated from each other—all their bowls and baskets and pans. Fortunately, the virus doesn't live very long outside the body. Ordinary household cleaners and disinfectants, like bleach, will keep the environment safe. That is, if the damage hasn't already been done. Kittens are particularly vulnerable if the maternal antibodies— the mother's transmitted immunity—have started to wear off and the cat hasn't built up his own. Which the little kitty probably hasn't. On the other hand, if the maternal immunity has worn off, he'll have to be vaccinated right away. Once again, if it's not too late."

They looked stricken.

"Bring the little guy in at once. I'll have to test him for FeLV—two tests, to be absolutely sure. If he's negative, we can start a series of vaccinations to immunize him."

"Tomorrow morning, then," said Edda.

Patch stepped obediently into his basket and off they went. Tiger came in the next day. To everyone's relief, he tested negative, and I gave him his first FeLV shot. He was not safe yet by any means, but at least we had started arming him against the deadly virus. As the days passed, Patch seemed to be holding steady. Edda and Frank did all they could to keep the two cats apart. It was virtually impossible, though, because Tiger seemed to be besotted with the older fellow and sought him out wherever he was. Patch would look at him benignly and whack him lightly with a gentle paw. It was almost heartbreaking to see how much Tiger loved him. Three weeks after his first FeLV vaccination, I gave tiny Tiger his second shot.

"He's looking good," I told Edda. "A zesty little fellow."

The Lombardis were learning the hard way just how dangerous it can be to take in a stray without knowing its history. The cat might be incubating a host of disorders, from internal parasites to the worst of the feline infectious diseases. It may have been inoculated against them or it may not; you can't know what its vaccination program has been. The only way to introduce a cat like Patch into a household with other cats is to keep it completely isolated from the others and get it to the vet as soon as possible to have it tested for infectious diseases, such as FeLV and FIV—feline immunodeficiency virus—and keep it separate for at least two weeks to let any lurking symptoms appear. If no disease shows up, the animal should be inoculated.

Patch was still holding steady, but he was quiet and his strength seemed sapped. We maintained the symptomatic treatment, but he no longer appeared to be responding positively.

Finally, the Lombardis and I agreed that this could not keep up much longer. Patch and Tiger, when they did accidentally get together, were simply not good for each other. The affection between them was evident and touching, but the kitten was a little bit too rambunctious for the older guy, and Patch was a minefield of infection.

And yet Edda and Frank and Tiger loved him. We had to ask ourselves: Was there any point in helping the older cat hang on? For what? He was getting worse. If he were alone with the Lombardis, they would love and nurse him as long as possible. But Tiger was still in danger, and it would be twelve weeks before I could give him the third shot of his injection cycle. Again, it was an agonizing choice.

With tears, it was decided to say farewell to Patch.

He died very peacefully in Edda's arms.

The remaining question was: Would Tiger be saved?

Tiger was puzzled and uncharacteristically subdued. For days he looked for his big buddy. There was no guarantee that he hadn't already been infected, that he was going to be all right. The weeks before he had that third shot were a nerve-wracking time for Edda and Frank. With Tiger's third shot—and he would be getting a booster every year—we began to feel more secure. And finally we knew for sure. He was a superbly healthy cat.

I'm not saying that everybody did everything right. The Lombardis led with their hearts; they lost something and they won something, and they learned something about strays.

Tiger will be nine years old this year. He is no longer a little round ball of fluff. He is a big round ball of fluff whose hobbies are chasing anything that moves and eating and picking fights with his adopted sister Sadie. He is as playful as ever. And he is the Big Guy now.

I guess the moral of this story is: Be very careful of the strangers you are tempted to let in and have them thoroughly checked up right away. They may be lovable but deadly; they may love their housemates to death. And you will mourn them anyway.

CHAPTER FOUR

Alley Cats
and Aristocrats

I'LL ALWAYS REMEMBER HER THAT WAY, beautiful Buttercup, sitting in the sunlight with her silver coat gleaming, admiring herself and being admired. Her story starts in the beginning of February in a long-ago year. My daughter Leslie's seventh birthday was coming up on April second, and my wife and I were hard pressed to find a present for her. We still had plenty of time, but we like to start worrying early and often. Eventually we decided we had a clue. Leslie had been asking for a cat for the past two years. We had told her that when she was old enough to help in the care of the cat, we would get her one.

Now, we thought, was the ideal time.

This was not to be a surprise; we wanted her to make her own choice. So, of course, being conscientious parents, we turned the process into a learning experience. We browsed through cat magazines, went to the library to take out books on breeds of cats and earnestly discussed them with Leslie. She looked at the pictures, patiently listened to my lectures and compared the various prospects with her friends' cats.

There were several cats that appealed to her from the start. Unfortunately, our research turned up so many new choices that it was difficult for her to settle on any single one.

So we looked and we looked, and I remembered cats I had known and loved, and I couldn't for the life of me say that any particular breed was preferable to another. There are over forty fairly distinct breeds, with many different types among them, and I would say that we have seen more than two hundred varieties of cats in the clinic—not all of them frequently, but enough of them often enough for me to have decided long ago that there is no such thing as the best kind of cat in the world. In all these years, I have scarcely ever met a cat I didn't like.

We decided that we had to narrow the field and concentrate on ten of the most popular breeds, after which we could focus on details of marking and color.

The most popular breeds we were seeing in the clinic at that time were the Domestic or American Shorthair, the Siamese, the Persian, the Russian Blue, the Abyssinian, the Maine Coon cat, the Manx, the Burmese, the Himalayan and the Havana Brown.

The Domestic Shorthair, sometimes known as the alley cat, is one of the oldest breeds. "Domestic" depends on where you are: This breed is seen all over, in the streets of Istanbul or Paris or New York City. It is the universal cat, the majority cat; in numbers alone, it is the number one cat in the world. You see these smart, tough survivors wherever you travel. I've seen them in restaurants in Paris, in the marketplaces of Turkey, on the grounds of the palaces of St. Petersburg, in the narrow alleys of Venice, in the kitchens of Ireland, in the barns of Vermont and Virginia, in the Mom-and-Pop stores of New York City and in the White House, too. Not that I've been there myself, but presidents from Lincoln to Clinton have kept them. What I think is so wonderful about them is that you can go around the world and know them instantly. You may not be able to speak the language of the people, but you can talk to the domestic cats. They have no outstanding distinguishing features, other than their resilience and ubiquity, yet they are quintessential Cat.

"Oh, but Daddy, they're ordinary. Just old yard cats."

But good-looking, smart, adaptable and fun.

Once, when visiting the Greek Isles, I stayed on the island of Hydra at a small inn that was built over two hundred years ago and is still owned by the founding family. When Jane and I were there, the proprietors had six rooms that they rented out; they also, coincidentally, had six cats of the Domestic Shorthair kind—all related, but in many different colors and designs. Every morning the owner of the inn got up at about six or six-thirty and greeted the cats in her small garden behind the house. Her routine was to put out three bowls of fresh yogurt and honey, and the cats would tuck in, two to a bowl, in a most polite and gentle manner—no pushing, no shoving, no boarding-house reach. To me, it was a novel and somehow touching scene. Each cat would dip a delicate paw into the bowl, lift it out drenched in honey and yogurt and lick off the yummy mix with silent pleasure. I took to watching morning after morning, and the routine never varied.

Apart from the nouvelle breakfast, the cats were fed on the regular home cooking emerging from the inn's wonderful kitchen, plus, I suppose, fairly frequent mouse snacks in between. They were about the healthiest, most beautifully muscled and alert cats I have ever met, and among the most beguiling.

Just ordinary, common garden cats. But not really ordinary at all.

Domestic Shorthairs in general are average-sized, that is, approximately eight to ten pounds. They are strong, hardy cats, street-smart if they are on the streets, and frisky but good-natured as pets. As hunters and mousers and watchcats, they are the prime working cats of the world. Plain and fancy, they wear coats of many colors and patterns. Perhaps the best known are black-and-white tuxedo cats, like President Clinton's cat, Socks, and the wide range of tabbies in black and silver, shaded red, tortoiseshell and calico.

A few things of interest about tabbies: A tabby is not a female cat, as loose talk would have us think—as in, "Oh, listen to those old tabbies, gossiping again." It is true that in some tabby colorings, the variety may be almost exclusively female or almost exclusively male, but the overall tabby population is about evenly split between the sexes. The word describes the markings, a striped and mottled effect over most of the body, with round dots, called buttons, on the tummy and a jewel-like design on the forehead between the eyes. This overall pattern is not exclusive to them; many so-called purebred or pedigreed cats have tabby markings, and one can only guess how that came about.

Siamese cats, one of the best known of the breeds, come and go on the popularity list. In the past twenty-five years or so they have been bred for one special look or another, and the extremely long and lithe look that breeders seem to fancy is not always a big hit with the public. But they are still a favorite in many cat-oriented households because they are interesting and different but not nearly so outlandish as some of today's custom-design cats. They're active, they're slim and svelte, they have a model's body; they can weave in and out of the narrowest places . . . that is, until they get along in years, when some of them are no longer quite so slim and svelte. But they are always elegant.

To describe and identify the different types of Siamese, you have to know about points. The points are the darker areas of the cat's body that appear on the head, ears, legs, paws and tail. Based on the point system, there are four recognized types of purebred Siamese cats: the Seal-point, which has seal-brown points and a fawn body; the Blue-point, which has deep silver paws and a gray body; the Lilac-point, which has pinkish points with a white body; and the Chocolate-point, which has chocolate points and an ivory body. All the Siamese have blue eyes. There are variations of the above four, and they are all quite lovely if you like the look.

What is really distinctive about the Siamese is that they have a built-in liking for heat. More than most cats, they like to lie in the sun or stretch out alongside radiators. Several I have known have enjoyed sleeping in the pool of hot light at the base of table lamps, looking like the morning-after life of the party. This is not markedly unusual among cats, but what is notable is that the temperature at which the Siamese are maintained directly influences their color. All Siamese emerge white or creamy white, including the points, from the warmth of the womb. It is only as the weeks and months go by and the cats become attuned to the relative coolness of the out-of-body experience that the darker shade of the points gradually becomes dominant. Thus it might be said that the dark areas represent cool temperatures and the light areas represent warmth.

A caveat: When selecting a Siamese, note that the most attractive and desirable Siamese do not have crossed eyes or kinky tails. These features are present quite often, but they are neither particularly glamorous nor, contrary to some notions, characteristic of purebreds.

Another caveat: They are the most talkative of cats. Many of them meow much of the time, often loudly, and there are people who find their vocalizing difficult to put up with or explain.

Some time ago, a client of mine moved from her house in Scarsdale, a suburb of New York, to an apartment in the city. She owned three Siamese cats, two Blue-points and one Lilac-point. All three cats had kinked tails, and one of the Blue-points was cross-eyed. Thus they were less than aristocratic cats, but they were royal loudmouths.

Mrs. Lynch didn't realize just how talkative her cats were when she moved into the building on East Sixty-fourth Street. It was her habit to feed the cats in the morning at about seven A.M. and leave for work at eight-thirty, so that the three Siamese were alone and chatting together until she came home from the office.

People living in apartments in New York City sometimes live right next door to their neighbors for years without knowing them or what they're like or whether or not they're married with children. Mrs. Lynch's neighbor had no idea who lived in the adjacent apartment. He was, as Mrs. Lynch described him after their first meeting, a crotchety old man and a real complainer. He would claim that he heard loud wailing every day, a chorus of misery that practically never stopped.

Sitting alone during the day and hearing the cries from next door, Mr. Hubbell wove a story in his mind that the sounds were the cries of children and that Mrs. Lynch was a bad mother who had left her babies all alone. The poor infants would cry all day until Mommy came home.

He apparently knew as little about children as he did about cats. I mean, what does a truly unhappy child sound like? How could all the children be infants at the same time? Watching television most of the day, Mr. Hubbell became obsessed by the wailings of the neglected babies in the apartment next door. And one day, by coincidence, he tuned into a program about abandoned children. It was then that he decided for certain that the crying voices were those of young children, infants, left home alone, hungry, while the mother absented herself for the day.

He was so moved by his own conclusion that he got on the telephone to the Children's Aid Society to complain about the conditions next door. As Mrs. Lynch's luck would have it, the Children's Aid Society came to investigate the situation at about seven o'clock that evening when she was home and feeding her babies. The investigators, of course, found out that the noisemakers were just three four-footed loudmouths.

Mrs. Lynch was furious and embarrassed, torn between anger at Hubbell's misguided interference and the sense that, if the situation had been different, he might well have been doing the right thing. And so, for a while, there was resentment and shame on both sides, but the episode started a relationship between Mrs. Lynch and her crusty neighbor. They eventually became good friends, and the cats continued to gossip all day.

Leslie wasn't all that interested in loud, skinny cats. She wanted to know about the fluffy Persian.

Well, then. The Persian is a contrary kind of cat. It hardly talks at all, and its body is so profusely covered with hair that it's hard to tell how lean and lithe it may or may not be. Yet Persian cats have been among the most popular of all breeds since Victorian times. Though somewhat scowly-looking, they are gentle of disposition and make affectionate pets. Very decorative, too.

But their beauty is also their curse. Their flowing long hair is subject to tangles and matting if not groomed frequently. This just takes a few minutes of combing out each day. If you start when the kitten is young, you'll find that the cat enjoys this and looks forward to being combed. Lots of Persians will just relax and let their owner groom them, purring away and wearing a blissed-out look on their snubby faces.

Uncombed Persians, on the other hand, are not happy cats. I've had many of them come into the office with a history of constant rubbing up against doors, walls, furniture, carpeting and anything else that doesn't move, quite clearly feeling very uncomfortable and looking terrible. I think that many of these cats had never been combed or brushed in their entire lives. People often don't realize that a cat like this needs special grooming; nobody ever told them. But as the cats lick themselves and their hair gets wet, it has a tendency to become matted. Sometimes the mats become more than an inch thick, at which point they can't be combed out. You can't even separate the fur. It's just a dense layer of hair, firmly attached to the skin.

Without clipping, these thick mats irritate the skin, and sores develop under the mats. When someone brings a cat into our office with this problem, we always suggest that the cat be clipped. It's the only way to get rid of the clumps and clean up the skin. And when the owners come and pick the cat up after this is done, they invariably say, "Is that my cat? That can't be my cat! What did you do to him?!" Because, of course, the cat looks completely different when devoid of all hair. And, of course, the owners must now take on the task of daily grooming as the hair grows in.

Persian cats come in many colors, from solids and shades of solid black to parti-colors like tortoiseshell or calico. They make very good pets, though subject to certain abnormalities like congenital entropion, which is an inversion of the eyelid. When this is present, the eyelashes rub against the cornea of the eye, irritating it and causing excessive tearing. This happens mostly in the lower lid and can be corrected successfully with surgery. These cats are also subject to stud tail, a greasy discharge at the base of the tail that can be cured most of the time by neutering the male and medicating the area.

"Too much work," said Leslie, her attention wandering. "How about this smoky blue cat?"

"It's a Russian Blue, a nice easy cat," I said. "It may not be Russian at all, but I sort of like the story that it was originally called Archangel Blue after the Russian port from which the cats were supposedly sent to Britain in the 1600s or maybe 1800s—it's hard to know when or where a particular breed actually originated. Whatever—the Russian Blue by any name is a beautiful animal with a slender body and short, plushy, blue hair tipped with silver, soft and silky to the touch. The nose and paw pads are also blue, and the eyes are a vivid green."

"A blue nose!" said Leslie, quite diverted. "Blue paws!"

"Unusual," I agreed. "The Blue I know best is a British-born cat by the name of Earl Grey, a rather princely-looking, self-possessed chap with an affectionate disposition who is totally devoted to his ten-year-old owner. In fact, Blues are said to be very good with children. I think that means that they're patient. All in all, this is a very attractive, low-maintenance cat."

Next on our list was the Abyssinian, one of the oldest breeds. As the story goes, "Abbys" were introduced to the West in the late 1860s by British soldiers returning home from the Abyssinian War. They are a slender cat, very attractive; they have short hair and come in a variety of colors. The Ruddy Abby has a reddish tail and a rich orange-brown coat, and the Red, or Sorrel, Abby has a deep red coat. Abbys also come in other colors—blue, fawn, lavender, silver and chocolate. In all cases, the coat is very beautiful and striking, and the fur is soft and silky.

Muscular, lithe, medium-sized cats, Abbys have an elegant look but a playful and friendly manner. They are intelligent and inquisitive cats who, for the most part, get along well with people and other animals. There are, of course, exceptions, as I learned later from personal experience.

Leslie liked the Abby; she also liked the totally different Maine Coon cat—a big, long-haired cat that has the distinction of being the oldest natural breed in North America. Its ancestors were probably Persian, as its long, soft coat, neck ruff and woolly tail suggest, but it has evolved into an all-American down-home cat, active and muscular. Some Maine Coons are scarcely more than medium-sized, but the male can weigh up to eighteen pounds and the female almost as much. Colors vary; they may be black as a black bear, ruddy as a raccoon, multi-colored like a long-haired tabby, almost any color other than chocolate or lavender. These are strong cats that like to hunt rodents and may even have gone to sea as ratters in earlier times. They're amiable, affectionate, good with children, tolerant of other animals, easy to train, still excellent rat-catchers and mousers, outdoorsy adventurers—which gives me my only reservation. I think they belong in the country.

"We live in the country," Leslie observed.

"Yes, but we don't encourage our animals to explore the woods."

Still, a cat will adapt; a cat will adapt from a mansion surrounded by woodsy acres to a tiny studio apartment, much better than people.

Now here was something entirely different: the Manx cat, known as the tailless cat, because indeed it does not have a tail. (This is not as obvious as it seems. The Sphynx is known as a hairless cat—but it does have hair.) The whole truth is that only the true Manx, known as the Rumpy, has absolutely no tail at all. Other Manxes have various degrees of tail and are variously known as Risers, Stumpies and Longies. They hail from the Isle of Man and have the rare feline distinction of appearing on the coinage of that land. They're lovely cats, strongly built, with handsome, sturdy bodies that are in no way diminished by the lack of a rear appendage. In the totally tailless Rumpy, there is a little furry hollow where the tail would normally begin. How it became tailless has been the subject of folklore since the first Manx was spotted, one theory being that it caught its tail in the door of Noah's Ark.

Rump aside, the Manx is distinguished by its glossy double coat: a short, compact underlayer covered by a longer, coarser topcoat. The visible coat comes in a variety of colors and patterns from solid white to red striped. In terms of personality, the Manx is a lovable, long-lived, intelligent cat.

"Well, I want a cat with a tail," said Leslie.

"Okay, let's try this one."

Together we looked at a full-page picture of a Burmese cat with its characteristic sable-brown coat, very short but rich as satin, and widely spaced yellow-gold eyes. There's a little echo of Siam in this cat, but the body and head are more rounded and the vocalizing is minimal. These, again, are lovable cats: sociable, but enormously loyal to their people, affectionate and totally beguiling. Even their facial expression is sweet. They make wonderful pets and are great with children.

This is hard. *All* these cats seem to be wonderful. Here is another: the Himalayan. It is a longhaired cat that looks so much like the Persian that it practically *is* Persian. In fact, its heritage is a cross of Persian and Siamese, with the Siamese aspect evident only in the points. It is a sweet-natured, quiet and cuddly cat with a coat like a soft, thick cloud—which has to be carefully groomed every day. And I don't think this should be left to a child.

A cat like the Havana Brown is easier. Characteristically, it is a rich chestnut brown in color, although some say it is more like a Havana cigar—even in its leanness. Here is another cat that owes something to the ubiquitous Siamese, in this case quite a lot. The body is streamlined yet muscular, the forehead wide, the nose long, the muzzle narrow but rounded. The kittens are born with blue eyes, which later turn a sparkling, almost mesmeric green and appear to be constantly on the alert. This is a lively, friendly cat that, more than most I've seen, tends to sit around with one raised paw as if deep in thought or about to shake a hand. In my experience, it has very few medical problems. In sum, another nice cat. Very intelligent, very affectionate, not very vocal; an active and playful pet.

While the entire family was engaged with the question of choosing Leslie's cat, a client of mine by the name of Milan Greer dropped by at my clinic one day for a consultation about his animals. Milan was one of the largest cat breeders in New York City, and I had often worked with him. I idly mentioned trying to help my daughter choose a cat; and he, more professionally, idly happened to mention one of his queens, a cat who had just given birth to two rather rare kittens. The queen was an unusual breed, a Silver Abyssinian—that is, unusual for the 'seventies. The Silver Abby is a trim-looking shorthaired cat whose coloring is very much like that of a chinchilla, pearly gray and somehow glowing, and whose personality is as alert and inquisitive as any other Abby.

Not long afterwards I had to make a house call to Milan's cattery to see several of his cats with various problems. While I was there, he showed me the Silver Abby and the two Abby kittens, who now were four weeks old. He told me he'd just sold the male to Henry Ford in Detroit for what struck me as a truly phenomenal price. The kitten would be flown to Michigan in about three or four weeks when it was old enough to travel.

I thought the Silver Abby was the loveliest cat I had ever seen, and the kittens looked like silver powder puffs, very appealing little creatures. I admired them appropriately, and thought to myself that if they weren't so enormously costly, my daughter might just like to take a look . . .

We were walking back to Milan's office when he said, to my huge surprise, "How about the sister of the Ford cat for Leslie? She'd like her, don't you think? I'd like to give it to you as my gift to Leslie because you've taken such fine care of all my animals for all these years. Please."

I thought of what Henry Ford was paying, and I blanched inside. Could I take this kind of gift?

But Leslie had no qualms. She was thrilled when I told her.

The decision was made. Leslie was going to get a Silver Abby.

So much for all our research; so much for having her choose.

But we had lucked in. Milan had made it easy. I didn't have to go on searching for the ideal kitten, and we—that is, Leslie—would be getting a really special cat from an ideal place.

I have always felt that the best way to go about getting a purebred animal is to find a respectable breeder, an honest breeder with healthy kittens, by looking in the Yellow Pages, in the local newspapers and in the back of magazines devoted to cats. Or, if it's just a really nice everyday kitty you're looking for, check out the kittens advertised for sale by private families, or go to a good shelter where the cats are cared for and have a clean environment.

The advantage of going to a breeder, or to a private family where you can meet the mother and father cats, is that you can see how the kittens will look and behave when they are fully grown adults. You can play with the parents and see what their personalities and dispositions are like, and also judge their temperaments. And the advantage of going to a good shelter is that the cost is very little. Most often it's just a donation for adopting a cat that might otherwise never find a home.

So on the April birthday, we gave Leslie a Silver Abyssinian. She decided to call it Buttercup, we having recently seen *H.M.S. Pinafore* and Leslie having fallen in love with the Buttercup name.

Buttercup grew up to be a beautiful, aristocratic cat. She liked to sit up on the back of the best living room chair, where the sun came through the windows and was nice and warm as it fell on her. She knew she was beautiful and loved to be admired. Everyone who saw Buttercup said, "You have to breed her, because I want one of her kittens." We must have had fifty requests.

When she was about two years old, we decided to breed beautiful Buttercup. I called a client who had a male Silver Abby.

Now Buttercup was very friendly with people, but we found out in a hurry that she didn't like male cats. We introduced her to her future husband, and she put on a performance you would never believe. She hissed, arched her back, stood on her toes and looked ready for war. We tranquilized her when she was in heat and put her in a large kennel with the stud cat. She stayed in the corner with her rear against the wall and refused to move. She wouldn't eat, she wouldn't drink, she wouldn't cooperate. We left her in the kennel with the male Abby for several days with no results.

We tried it again the next time she was in heat, giving her a slightly larger dose of the tranquilizer and a little more time. Nothing worked. She put on the same performance. We were obliged to give up on poor little Buttercup. She was one frigid cat, a determined virgin, and there was nothing we could do about it.

So much for supplying our friends with adorable silver kitties.

Because of our inability to get her bred, and for health reasons, we decided to spay this lovely cat. Unspayed cats that are not bred tend to develop uterine infections, and it was much safer to spay her while she was healthy.

Buttercup turned out to be the exception to the rule that Abbys love people, other animals and having a good time. She adored Leslie, who adored her in return, but I rather suspect that she loved herself best. And so Buttercup spent the rest of her life being admired, perched up high on a chair in the sunshine where she could be viewed by everyone.

When my daughter Betsy reached the age of seven, she decided that she, too, wanted a cat she could call her own. Betsy, however, didn't want an aristocratic cat like Buttercup; she wanted a kitten she could cuddle, and she didn't want to look through a lot of books. One Sunday afternoon in May, we were invited to a picnic at a friend's house, where there were several families and many children. One little girl told Betsy about her cat that had just had five kittens, of which her mother would only let her keep one.

So there were four kittens looking for good homes. Betsy and her friend arranged for us to see the kittens as soon as the picnic was over.

When Betsy saw the kittens, she immediately picked out the red-and-white one, a Domestic Shorthair—in other words, an alley cat.

Six weeks after that, we took home the little calico.

Betsy, another Gilbert and Sullivan fan, named her YumYum.

YumYum grew up to be just the opposite of Buttercup. She was outgoing and couldn't wait to be hugged and petted and played with. The two of them tolerated each other but never really got along. Any time YumYum attempted to make a friendly gesture, Buttercup would hiss and stalk away.

So we wound up with a princess and a plain little yard cat.

Today I might consider a Tonkinese or a Bobtail or a Ragdoll or one of the Rex breeds or a Birman or a Mau or an Ocicat or a Chartreux or a Bombay . . . so many wonderful cats to choose from! But I'm not likely to advise anyone to get a particular breed of cat—an Abyssinian, for example, even though I love them—on the grounds that it's going to be affectionate or playful or lively or intelligent. Whatever the breed, whatever its alleged characteristics, a cat is an individual. It's going to be what it's going to be, and not what you or I planned for it.

CHAPTER FIVE

Mating Game

WHEN PAWLINE WAS STILL NO BIGGER than a squirrel, the Gardners moved from their low-rise apartment building to a small townhouse abutting others. In a block-long row of buildings, it was hard to distinguish one from the other until you happened to go out back and see the little yards. Some were peaceful sanctuaries with careful plantings, birdbaths and climbing roses, mini-oases to soothe the frazzled spirit. Others were dominated by wooden decks and barbecue equipment. One or two were jungles of weeds. A few looked comfortable and lived-in. The Gardners' place was one of these.

It had a small deck hovering over a patch of earth sprouting low-lying swatches of grass, which they called their lawn and mowed heroically. In the spring, the flower beds lining the fences were a dazzle of daffodils and tulips, in spite of the squirrels that periodically lunched on the bulbs, but for most of the year, the garden effects relied on hanging plants, banks of ivy and a few determined rose bushes that struggled against too much shade and too little fertilizer. On the other side of the stockade fence that separated their property from the house behind them was a chicken coop, one of whose occupants woke up the entire neighborhood at dawn's earliest light with the traditional cock-a-doodle-doos. Nancy swore the back neighbors were breeding fighting cocks; John just swore. In time they got used to the rural sound and even became rather proud of it. "Is this New York or *what?*" they would ask triumphantly.

Their neighbors to either side were slightly more conventional than the chicken people—youngish couples with youngish children and a variety of pets, all of whom spent considerable time in their little squares of nature. Pawline, equipped with a red collar and a heart-shaped ID tag, took one look at the great outdoors and instantly became an indoor-outdoor cat, prowling the immediate neighborhood and getting to know its more important features: how the other cats lived, which ones were allowed out and which weren't, where she could get a free snack between meals (elderly gardening-type lady three houses along), nasty boy (to the rear and one house over), dog as big as a pony (four fences down) and the two-year-old girl twins two gardens away. Pawline liked the little girls best of all.

Being as unreasonable as most cats, Pawline took a one-sided view of the territorial question. She assumed the right to explore other people's yards and poke her nose into every nook and cranny, but the cat who dared to walk along the top of her fence or stroll through her yard or venture onto her deck was in very deep trouble indeed. The nearby yards were her beat; her immediate territory was hers, *hers!* and she let all trespassers know it with arched and bristling back and fearsome howls and hisses. Nancy didn't especially mind the incursions. She thought they were all nice kitties. But when the altercations escalated into screaming matches, she felt obliged to intervene. Her best weapon, she soon learned, was a long-barreled water gun, much like the type of thing known these days as a Super Soaker, which she aimed at Pawline and intruder alike. It was so effective in breaking up quarrels that she began to use it, with similar success, on bulb-hunting squirrels.

Weeks became months, and Pawline rounded into a budding adolescent. When Nancy brought her in for her rabies vaccination, I reminded her that it was perilously close to the time for the cat to be spayed, since Pawline's freewheeling lifestyle might tend to lead her to early motherhood.

"No, I'm going to keep her indoors for a while," said Nancy. "We'd like to breed her just once, but not to one of the neighborhood ruffians, and keep a kitten or two. Then we'll, uh, fix her."

"Suits me," I said. "Wait till her second heat to breed her, when she's a little more mature mentally and physically. So what ruffian would you prefer?"

"I thought from that farm where we got her? Maybe she has a handsome cousin or something."

"Maybe. But best not wait much longer, or you might be sorry."

"Well, I don't know," she said. "Isn't it true that it's a good thing to let a cat have a litter first? Let her live a little? Isn't it supposed to improve a cat's personality?"

I glared at her, I really did. "That is a rumor and nothing but a rumor," I said with mock severity. "I don't know what Old Wife started it, but there is not a syllable of truth in it. Neither the cat's health nor the personality is improved. The opposite, if anything, is closer to the truth. Besides, there is absolutely no need to improve Pawline's personality."

Nancy looked slightly abashed. "I guess the truth is that I want to see her with kittens. I want to see what they look like and how she is with them."

"Well, that's okay if you're positive you'll find homes for them. If you knew how many unwanted cats are put to death every year, you wouldn't think so much about personality improvement."

"They're not going to be unwanted," Nancy said firmly. "I want them. I'll find homes. Then you can spay her. Oh, and what did you mean, I might be sorry if I waited?"

"Some people can't stand the racket," I said.

"Racket?"

She gave me one of her really blank looks, and once again I had to explain some of the facts of life. I told her about Mrs. Reed and the Siamese cat her son Jarvis had given her.

"Mrs. Reed is a widow," I began, "who was very lonely after her husband's death. So her son Jarvis decided to get her some company. He had two cats of his own, and he knew his mother was very fond of them. So he presented this cat to her on her sixty-fifth birthday, and she was thrilled. He told her that the cat was four months old, in excellent health, had had all of its vaccinations and a complete checkup by his own veterinarian and was free from worms and all kinds of parasites. All she had to do was feed and water it and give it tender loving care, which he knew his mother would do. I guess she knew it was a female, because she called it Annie.

"About two months later, she called me, on the recommendation of one of my good clients, and told me about her birthday gift. Up to this time, she said, everything had been just fine. The cat was adorable, faithful and affectionate. She was nuts about it. Everything about Annie indicated that the kitty was in perfect health—everything but just one thing. She had begun to howl. First thing in the morning, Mrs. Reed was being awakened by these loud, really penetrating meows, which Annie had never produced before. She—the cat—ate, slept, washed herself and used her litter pan normally, but she seemed to be screaming for help. Something was causing her terrible pain. But Mrs. Reed didn't want to tell her son that the cat was in agony and probably dying, so she had called me.

"Well, that, of course, is what I'm here for. We had a full schedule that morning, but she seemed so distressed I felt I had to tell her we would fit her in as soon as she could get here. Which we did. There was, as I had suspected, nothing wrong with the cat."

"So what's your point?" said Nancy. "Something wrong with the lady?"

"Of course not," I said. "What was happening with this little female was simply nature taking its course. She was in heat. At six months old. I put her on the examination table, and she howled like a banshee. And kept howling. She had her tail elevated, and her vulva was enlarged. I explained this to Mrs. Reed, but it seemed to mean nothing to her. She said she had no experience with this sort of thing. I told her the cat was in estrus and at this time was sexually receptive to the male. Mrs. Reed seemed to be quite shocked."

"Naturally, who wouldn't be?" said Nancy, lifting Pawline's tail and peeking under it. Pawline gave an offended little squawk. We were through with her for the day, and she knew her routine. "And what," Nancy asked, "is the moral of this story for me?"

"There is no moral, merely a point. The point being that when the female cat is sexually mature and gets into the mating mood, she is going to start howling. It really does sound as if the cat is in pain, even though she isn't. Male cats know that. They're out there some place, listening, coming over the fences and into the yard, snooping around the doors and windows, watching, waiting, beating off other local toms attracted by her cries . . . "

I was getting carried away.

"And the climax usually is—exactly that," I wound down. "A meeting takes place between the queen and a stud, there will be kittens, there will be another heat period, another meeting, and so it goes."

"So what's to be done?" said Nancy.

"If you don't want kittens, you keep your cat in the house, and you take your water gun and blast the boys out of the yard. Of course, they'll come back, and meanwhile, the female will keep on howling. Furthermore, she's going to keep it up for days and start all over again in a few weeks or maybe sooner. And some of the females get very, very noisy. Like Mrs. Reed's Annie. Also the males fight a lot."

"A sad situation," said Nancy. "So what happened about Mrs. Reed's cat?"

"Mrs. Reed didn't want kittens. We decided to spay her cat. She wanted it done right away because she couldn't stand the howling. She said it was driving her mad."

"That bad, huh?" Nancy said thoughtfully. "Okay, I may be sorry, but I do want to see one litter first. I want to watch her nurse them and enjoy them. And gradually give them away. Oh, by the way— how was Annie's personality after the operation?"

"Transformed," I said firmly. "No more howling, except for the usual Siamese arias. Even more loving than before, and the absolute essence of charm. Adorable."

"How nice," said Nancy. "I still want Pawline to be a queen."

Nancy and Pawline, intact, went home together.

Good luck, I thought. Sometimes the first couple of rounds aren't really so bad.

The female cat may come into heat for the first time as early as five months of age, the average age of onset being six or seven months. The heat period, or estrus, can occur as often as every two to four weeks and usually lasts about five days, though in some cases it seems to be virtually nonstop. Luckily, breeding time is limited to a mere eight or nine months of the year. From late September to the third week in December, both male and female cats tend to be in a more-or-less quiescent state. We were, at that point, nearing the end of March. Pawline's timing would no doubt be excellent.

Mrs. Gardner called a few weeks later.

"I can't stand it!" Nancy screamed. "This is not howling, it's *yowling!* She's running back and forth like a maniac, she's rolling on the floor, she's making passes at John, she's clawing at the doors and windows and trying to get out, and those tomcats are hollering, and it's driving me crazy."

I smiled a little smile and did not say "I told you so."

What I did say was: "Call that Catskills farmer you told me about and tell him you want to mate her when she's next in heat. Arrange to be there as soon as she goes into her next cycle—which will be soon, believe me. And then let her do whatever comes naturally."

Nancy groaned. In the background, I heard the piercing cry of a frustrated female cat. Pawline was definitely ready. I also said: "If it gets really bad, I usually advise my clients to try a little vodka and milk."

"Howzat?" said Nancy, rather faintly.

"Vodka for you, milk for the cat," I said helpfully. "And a tranquilizer for you both."

It was spring in the Catskills when the Gardners drove up the farmer's dirt road with their camping equipment on top of the car. Pawline had been yelling and rattling her cage all the way, and John and Nancy were speaking through very tight lips. "Definitely, never again," Nancy muttered.

The farmer smiled a welcome and, like a hospitable innkeeper, showed Pawline into a fresh-smelling barn well equipped with cat food and water in addition to the resident mice. Then he disappeared for a moment and came back with a macho-looking tomcat of a different color and similar markings. There was a distinctive black patch over one eye.

"We thought this one best matched your description," he said. "He's healthy, he's productive, he's handsome, and he performs. We call him the Marlboro Man."

John grunted. "What if she doesn't like this bozo?"

"He's always been found irresistible," the farmer said cheerfully, "but there's no shortage of studs around here. Just give them a couple of days in the barn together and see how they hit it off. I have to tell you, though—ninety-nine times out of a hundred, they do. She wants it."

"Oh, that's what men always say," sniffed Nancy. "And what about him? Is he in the mating mode, too?"

"He always is," said the farmer. "He is always ready. Just like women always say." He smiled and added, "Shall I put him in with her?"

Introductions completed inside the barn, the cats were left to themselves in a box stall. It would not take long for them to get to know each other. Meanwhile, Nancy and John pitched their tent in a meadow.

Later in the day, they strolled up to the barn.

"Say, there's a window," said Nancy. "Let's take a peek."

"Voyeur," said John, muscling her aside. They scuffled for position.

A terrible cry came from within.

"Omigod!" said Nancy. "Would you look at that!"

The stud approached Pawline from the side and bit into the nape of her neck. It seemed to the voyeurs like a vicious attack, but it always looks worse than it is. And sounds worse, too. The tomcat growled, Pawline snarled, Nancy gasped, and John said, "Wow!" By this time, the stud had placed his front legs over his mate's shoulders and mounted her so that his entire body was covering hers. She then arched her back and lifted her tail to one side, and mating took place. The entire episode took less than five minutes and ended with Pawline giving a mating scream and rolling out of the tomcat's grasp.

"Not a pretty sight," said Nancy.

"Well, it's what you wanted," said John. "For her, that is." Pawline, however, did not seem thrilled by the event. Turning on the stud with an ugly snarl, she threw herself at him and attacked with tooth and claw. Pulling away, the stud swarmed up a long, straight ladder, leapt onto a high shelf and disappeared behind a bale of hay. The bride gave one scrabbling leap up the ladder, slid down, then positioned herself at its base, waiting.

"Was that it?" Nancy asked.

"Some of it," said John. "My understanding is that they should stay together for at least another twenty-four hours. They keep mating five or six times a day."

Which, apparently, they did.

Throughout the weekend, occasional shrieks were heard from the barn, indicating either agony or ecstasy or both, but they were not fighting shrieks. It seemed as if the encounter, so roughly begun, had turned into a success.

It seemed even more likely when the lovers came out of the honeymoon suite, looking—Nancy said—sheepish but smug.

"Anthropomorphia strikes again," said John, bundling his females back into the car.

Pawline purred contentedly all the way home.

CHAPTER SIX

Backyard
Menageries

IT OCCURS TO ME THAT THERE IS SCARCELY A CAT to be
seen in this tale of a turtle, a couple of raccoons and a rabbit,
but if it weren't for the cat connection, I doubt if I would have
been involved in it at all. Yet there was a cat in the house next
door to Pawline's family, and that is what began it all for me.

Not many people outside of New York City realize what a collec-
tion of little communities our city is. It is true that there are sections
where people live on the same block or even in the same apartment
house for years and never meet or speak, but to my knowledge, these
are few. We have neighborhoods. Many of us even have front stoops

and small backyards with fences over which we talk—little worlds in microcosm. And some of these are enlivened by surprising menageries.

So it was with the backyard of the Randalls, next door to the Gardners, often visited by Pawline in the course of her rambles.

The Randalls had an indoor-outdoor cat named Elizabeth, a Portuguese water dog called Spritzer, Ozzie the white rabbit, who for the most part occupied a commodious outdoor cage but came indoors during bad weather, and a turtle known as Queenie. Her full name was Speed Queen, so dubbed by preteeners Holly and Ed Randall in their first foray into irony. The turtle was moderately large, maybe about the size of a large hand or medium foot, and it lived in a little pond in the yard with toys and furnishings of its own. One would have supposed it to be content with its lot, but apparently it was not.

Completing the cast of more or less full-time backyard occupants were several chattering squirrels and a committee of imitative blue jays that sounded uncannily like car alarms and police sirens—*heehaw-heehaw-heehaw, eeow-eeow-eeow*—the quintessential New York sound. More tuneful birds twittered from the trees in the mornings and evenings.

Elizabeth the cat, taking her ease on the minuscule patio, held court most days. According to Teri Randall, who told Nancy, the Randall backyard had become a meeting place for a number of quite well-mannered local cats who apparently just dropped by to converse and chew the neighborhood fat. There were no fights, no yowls or screams, just the purrs and mumbles of old acquaintances congregating for a chat. A few times, at dawn or dusk, a raccoon had been spotted, behaving in what seemed like a civilized manner, checking out the rabbit in its cage and cutting a fairly wide swath around the cats.

Then the raccoon disappeared. As did the turtle.

One day Teri came over to visit Nancy and Pawline. Teri was worried. She said, "This may sound silly, but I'm beginning to think that the turtle ran off with the raccoon."

Nancy said, "I think it's far more likely that the raccoon ran off with the turtle. You haven't seen any bits of turtle shell around? Maybe turtle is a raccoon's favorite dish—have you thought of that?"

"You're joking, of course! Aren't you?"

Somehow, through the neighborhood grapevine, word of the missing turtle and her suspected kidnapper came to the ears of a woman with a pet raccoon named Rocky. The woman telephoned Teri.

Jenny Hunt was horrified at the notion that her little cutie could possibly have had anything to do with the disappearance of Queenie. "He eats at home!" she said frantically. "What would he want with the turtle? Did anyone see him near the pool?"

"It's okay," Teri said soothingly. "Queenie probably decided to run away by herself. She's probably still crossing the road. Don't worry about it. I seriously don't think Rocky had her for dinner. It's more likely some kid picked her up."

"But he's acting strangely!" Jenny moaned. "Maybe he's sick! Maybe it's something he ate!"

Oh, please, Teri said to herself. To Ms. Hunt she said, "Then I think you should take him to the vet."

And that's how I get into these things.

Rocky was a feisty, energetic young fellow who seemed abundantly healthy to me. A little highly strung, perhaps, but certainly not atypical of his breed. Jenny Hunt, on the other hand, was very nervous. If, she asked, *if* he had actually carted off the turtle and tried to eat it, would that be bad for him?

"Not good for the turtle," I observed. "But let me say that I don't think there is a chance in a thousand that Rocky is guilty in this case. He's only about two months old, and he's much too small to capture a turtle. We're obviously talking about another, bigger raccoon. Rocky is off the hook."

Ms. Hunt looked relieved but not quite ready to go home.

I prompted her. Rocky'd already had all his shots before she got him? Right. Appetite always good? Oh, very good. And in what way was he acting strangely?

Ms. Hunt gave a little confessional sigh. "I think he's a teeny bit of a weirdo," she whispered. And added, "I guess maybe I am too."

I wasn't sure I wanted to hear this, but she went on.

"I had a little dog when I was a child," she said. "And it always slept on my bed. Sometimes at my feet, and sometimes under the covers. And then, when I brought Rocky home, he right away started coming to bed with me. He was so cute and cuddly, only four weeks old. In fact, he scratched my back at night, and I found it very soothing. I don't sleep well, and the scratching felt really good."

My goodness, I thought, this young woman is a little unusual. But she was trusting enough to tell me about it, so okay.

"And that's the problem," she said. "It's not soothing any more. It was lovely when he was just a tiny fellow, but now that he's larger, those little baby claws have grown into can openers, and he's scratching too hard. It really hurts. I actually bleed sometimes. And yet I don't want to throw him out of the bed and hurt his feelings. What am I to do?"

"Well, I don't think you'd hurt his feelings," I said. "I have, actually, yet to hear of an oversensitive raccoon. But it might be hard to break him of the habit of clawing you to pieces. I would suggest that if you really want him as a house pet, you have him neutered and declawed. He's at the age for it, and I think you'll both be happier."

As it turned out, I was wrong about the happiness part, but no one could have guessed it when she brought him in the following week for surgery.

Our plan was to keep Rocky overnight before starting operative procedures, giving him a chance to settle down and feel at ease with us. We took him from his owner's arms, and the technician on duty—Pablo, at that time—put him into a modern, stainless steel cage. Pablo turned his back. Rocky reached a skinny arm through the bars of the cage, opened up the door latch and leapt out.

We caught him after a while and bundled him back in, deciding to do the operations with minimal delay since he was obviously a born escape artist. After his operations, we would keep him for five days in a cage with a serious lock on the door.

First we nipped the claws. There's an ongoing controversy about declawing animals—is it being cruel to be kind, or is it just being cruel? I'm in favor of declawing for house cats, and it's an absolute necessity for domesticated raccoons. I don't personally believe that they should be kept as city house pets anyway, but if they are, they ought to live by house rules. And that means no clawing at owners, no noshing on other pets and no sex life. It's tough, but pet lovers ought to think about the quality of life for animals—especially wild animals—they bring under their roofs.

A raccoon's claws are about half an inch long but are rooted no more deeply than a cat's, so the declawing operations are virtually identical. Healing time is also about the same: ten days to removal of sutures, with care taken that no irritating substance enters the tiny wounds. And neutering, as with a male cat, is not major surgery, though it has impressive results.

A calmer and cooler Rocky went home with his mistress, who was thrilled with the change in him. After picking him up, she called a couple of times a week for the next three weeks to tell us how wonderful life with Rocky was. Then the calls began to dwindle, and finally stopped. All seemed to be well.

Early one morning, when my office was not yet officially open but the staff and I were checking our schedules for the day, Ms. Hunt burst in, screaming hysterically and holding the raccoon in her arms like an offering to us. "Look at him, look at him!" she cried. We did. "He's all cold and stiff!"

Indeed he was, stretched out and apparently lifeless. We took Rocky into our emergency room and gave him a rapid examination, ready to swoop into action with CPR and IVs and everything that modern veterinary medicine could offer. I knew in my heart it was already too late, but the least I could do was examine him. No heartbeat. Not a trace. Mucous membranes blue. We tried to resuscitate, but it was hopeless. Rocky was gone.

I couldn't understand it. Rocky had been one healthy raccoon when we had seen him last. I turned to Ms. Hunt.

"What happened?"

She was still hysterical, but she made some sort of sense.

"I don't let him out of the house anymore," she said. "He doesn't pick up anything on the outside. He doesn't have contact with any other animals. He still stays on the bed at night, but he doesn't scratch any more. And I still don't sleep well. I take pills. I had a bottle of Seconal on the bedside table. Early this morning, I woke up and saw them scattered all over the table and the floor, and Rocky was lying at the foot of the bed—out like a light! And now he's dead! Dead, dead, dead!"

"Did you by any chance gather up the pills and bring them with you?" "Yes," she said tearfully, thrusting the bottle at me. "Do you know how many pills you've taken?" I queried. "It was a new bottle—I only had two." The number of pills dispensed appeared on the label. "Let's count," I said. A quick dose of arithmetic showed that Rocky had popped ten of the powerful sedatives, far too many to permit a small creature to survive.

Ms. Hunt departed, weeping, deploring her negligence. "My fault," she moaned. "My fault."

She was right. It was. I didn't rub it in.

But after she had gone, I had the fleeting thought that maybe Rocky had simply given up on life. What did he have left? No claws, no sex, not even bedtime back scratches. No furry friends. No fun. And so he had ended it all.

I rebuked myself for this ridiculous notion, but I could not help the further thought that Ms. Hunt was not an ideal pet owner.

Meanwhile, back at the Randalls, Teri and her husband, Jeff, were worried about Ozzie the rabbit. There'd been no sign of the missing turtle, and there was certainly no reason to believe that Ozzie's problems had anything to do with Queenie. He just didn't look very well one day. When Jeff checked his cage one late afternoon after coming home from work, he saw that the rabbit hadn't touched any food, hadn't touched any water and looked quite listless. And when Jeff let him out of his cage for his evening romp, he didn't play with the other animals or with the kids. Ozzie was just out of it.

Jeff decided to isolate him overnight and keep a close watch on him. He brought Ozzie inside and put him in his bad-weather cage in a little room just off the kitchen, leaving him with a supply of fresh water and pellets. Every once in a while, he and Teri would look in on him and observe—nothing. Finally, they both slept.

Next morning they found Ozzie stretched out in his cage looking really ill and very sorry for himself. He had touched none of his food and water, and what was quite alarming was that he had had bloody diarrhea in the night.

Everyone else in the house was fine—animals, parents and kids as well. Jeff called me at the hospital and told me how sick the rabbit was. I said to bring him over right away.

Ozzie looked truly terrible. We examined him. His gums were almost white, instead of the normal pink, a sure sign of anemia. A blood test confirmed this. I had to tell Jeff that without a blood transfusion, we were going to lose Ozzie.

"A blood transfusion for a rabbit," he muttered. "I can't believe it. Is there a rabbit blood bank?"

"No, there isn't," I said. "But we'll try to manage."

Jeff left Ozzie in the hospital and raced off to work.

Now I had to think: Where was I going to get bunny blood?

Only from another rabbit.

I had about twenty clients with rabbits, all of them currently healthy and any of which would be a suitable donor. Blood type was not an issue. Within the cat world and the rabbit world, the blood type for each is pretty much constant. The overwhelming majority of American domestic cats have Type A blood. A minority of purebreds have the much rarer Type B, and a very small number of breeds and domestics have been found with the extremely rare AB. With rabbits, there was even less variation that I knew of. The odds were astronomical that any rabbit blood I could get hold of would be fine for Ozzie. *If* I could get hold of it, and soon.

I ran through my mental list of rabbit-owning clients. They were all very much attached to their pets, and I doubted that any one of them would be thrilled to have their rabbit's blood tapped. And yet it was just possible I might find someone who would think it worthwhile and perhaps even interesting.

While I was deliberating about which rabbit owner to call, I remembered that there was a live chicken market in an Italian neighborhood on the lower east side of Manhattan. Chicken markets also sell live rabbits. In fact, there were a number of these markets in Brooklyn and the Bronx, but the one in Manhattan would be most convenient for us.

I called the market and asked them if they had any live rabbits.

Oh, yes! They had plenty of rabbits. How many did I want?

I said just one would be fine for a start. There was a recipe I wanted to try out. So I ordered the largest rabbit they had, a two-and-a-half-pound white rabbit at seventy-five cents a pound, specifying that I wanted it *alive*. Then I sent one of my kennelmen down in a taxi, armed with a cat carrier, to pick up Ozzie's blood donor.

While waiting for the rescue party, my technician Liz and I took a sample of Ozzie's blood to get a blood count and a complete blood chemistry. It confirmed acute anemia. We also learned that Ozzie had acute hemorrhagic gastroenteritis, an infection of the gastrointestinal tract. This had probably come from something Ozzie had eaten in one of his recent gambols in the Randall backyard. And from a stool sample, we discovered that he also was infected with coccidiosis, a condition caused by a protozoan parasite in the intestinal tract that can cause blood loss. These two infections, gastroenteritis and coccidiosis, had caused Ozzie's anemia.

Now the question was: How did he get the coccidiosis parasite? It is not transferable from one species to another, so he couldn't have picked it up in the Randall yard. There were no other rabbits in the neighborhood. Ordinarily a rabbit contracts coccidiosis from another with the same disease, primarily through nosing around in feces. He ingests the eggs, which develop in the intestinal tract, and next thing you know, you have a rabbit with bloody diarrhea. But as Ozzie had no rabbit contacts, we figured this young fellow must have gotten it from his mother and brought it with him to the Randalls.

Ozzie was looking very pale indeed by the time the new rabbit arrived, seemingly almost comatose with fright himself. He was a fine, healthy fellow, though, and Liz soon calmed him down enough for us to make the blood transfusion. Ozzie was too tired and apathetic to realize that we had plugged yet another needle into his vein, but even as we watched, we could see the roses coming back into his gums.

Both Ozzie and our new rabbit made a complete and speedy recovery. Ozzie, of course, had to be returned to his owners. They were thrilled about the transfusion and grateful to the donor, but they didn't need another rabbit. So—what to do with our hero? I could scarcely send him back to the market. And though I did have a rabbit recipe, our new friend would have no part in it.

Liz, the technician who had helped with the transfusion, was hovering over me while I wondered out loud what to do with the donor bunny. "Well, um," she said, "I've gotten rather fond of him. I could take him home, couldn't I? Couldn't I adopt him?"

I knew her family—big, raucous, lots of kids, crazy about animals. The upshot was that she did take him home, and Ozzie and Eeyore lived happily ever after with their respective loved ones.

P.S. No one ever did solve the mystery of Speed Queen's disappearance, but there were further sightings of another non-Rocky raccoon. He'd progressed to knocking over garbage cans and plants and making a big nuisance of himself, to the point where one of the neighbors had him trapped and sent away. Did the remains of Queenie go with him? We'll never know.

CHAPTER SEVEN

Getting Along Like Cat *and* Cat

MOST PEOPLE ARE UNDER THE IMPRESSION that cats and dogs can't co-exist happily under the same roof. This belief is mostly held by people who own either a cat or a dog but not both, or a person who has never owned a pet at all. They may be right when it comes to wild dogs and wild cats on the same turf, but the reality is that domesticated cats and dogs are not natural enemies. In fact, if you start them young enough, cats can get along happily with any other creature . . . except maybe birds and tropical fish. I, personally, wouldn't want to put a cat and a bird or a goldfish together in my own household. Other people have, and they've made it work, but accommodations must be made.

The odd thing is, it's more common for a cat not to get along with another cat.

When my little girl Betsy demanded, and got, a cat of her own, there were already a couple of dogs in the Padwee household plus the glamorous Buttercup. Betsy's cat, YumYum, was about eight weeks old when we brought her home, and like a good many kittens I have known, she promptly started to attack all the furniture in sight. It was decided that she should be declawed; no sooner said than done. YumYum quit clawing the furniture, though she sometimes stretched herself against it and stroked the fabric as if she liked the feel of it on her paws, but she did no further damage and grew up to be an unspoiled, loving little cat.

Yet try as she might, she couldn't make friends with Buttercup. Buttercup was aloof and self-contained; YumYum was outgoing, loved to play, couldn't wait to be hugged and petted. Buttercup was a one-person cat and a one-cat cat. The one person was Leslie, who adored her and was adored in return, and the one cat was Buttercup herself.

Buttercup may even have been just a mite jealous of the younger cat. Whatever her hangup, she would hiss and stalk off whenever YumYum tried to give her a friendly sniff.

YumYum gave up trying after a while and made the most of life as she knew it. Claws or no claws, she used to run around outside the house, chasing down the neighborhood wildlife, and come back to the house bearing gifts—chipmunks and other rodents—which she would deposit on the doorstep. This, I thought, was a kindly gesture, because other cat owners are often gifted with mice on their pillows or even on their chests, and the worst YumYum did was leave them where we could step on them.

She had another and more endearing characteristic. For all that she couldn't charm Buttercup into liking her, she had the dogs in the palm of her paw. She would tease them into playing with her, and they loved it. Big William, the Golden Retriever, was her favorite playmate. Playing the game of Swallow the Cat, YumYum performed the death-defying role of maiden in distress being consumed by a dragon.

William, with his great big snapping jaw, took her tiny, vulnerable head into his big, toothy mouth and—so it seemed—clamped down on the little neck. Crunch!

Oohh! Squeals of delight from the children and gasps of horror from unwary adults as Big Willie gently swung her around. The Incredible Headless Cat! The Famous Disappearing Cat Trick!

YumYum loved it. She would go along with it for up to half an hour at a stretch sometimes, and I could swear she came out chirping and giggling, even though covered with dog drool. And never, never did I see Big William fasten his teeth on her or hurt or frighten her in any way. The Crunch! was all in the mind.

Multi-animal households can be full of surprises.

There is a family near where I live today that consists of two parents, four kids, a Weimaraner named Smoky, a cat, a parrot and a forty-five-pound Vietnamese potbellied pig called PigPig. There was a little difficulty for a time between the cat and the parrot, and both of them bear scarred witness to the strife, but the conflict was resolved by keeping the parrot cage on an enormously tall stand and getting the cat a pet of its own: PigPig. Rudy the pink-nosed cat actually shares his litter pan with the pig, which I would not have believed if I had not seen it with my very own eyes. Actually they take turns; but though it is a largish litter pan, PigPig is—a pig. And Rudy is very forgiving.

The only other problem with PigPig is that, unless she is watched very carefully, she tends to gobble up cat food and dog food on sight, and she is supposed to be on a permanent diet. Theoretically, she's a small pig, but even a small pig becomes a big pig if it eats like a—well—a pig.

PigPig has always had to have special food. These are not dwarf pigs, these potbellies; they really are pig pigs. So if such a pig is going to be kept around a home, particularly if it's going to be sharing a kitty pan, it has to have a small-piggy diet. It's essential not to let a pet pig get overweight. Left to eat with the others, PigPig has shown a powerful tendency to beat all the rest of them to the trough. If she should keep this up she would get too big to be an indoor pet. So she has to be fed her own clean, largely vegetarian meals in a separate room.

The cat, in its turn, will not and should not eat pig food, nor is she supposed to eat the dog's food, because it doesn't contain the right nutrition for cats. So she has to eat alone. The dog is fed separately so he won't eat his friends' food, which he tries to do, be it food for the parrot or the pig.

The Vietnamese potbelly is a nice house pet for some houses. Its appetite is none too easily curbed, but other than that, it is trainable and obedient. PigPig's training started when she was very young, say about two months or even a little younger. Her people have built a special platform for her so that she can go up and down stairs. Pigs climbing stairs? Something strange here. But she does it, and often Rudy the cat will join her. I don't think they know which one is the pig and which the cat.

The main point is, all the animals are healthy and apparently contented. All are great pals and get along as friends do. The pig kisses the cat, the cat nuzzles the pig's neck, the dog kisses everybody but the parrot, and the parrot nibbles gently at its people. These combinations tend to work very well, especially when there's no visiting raccoon.

And then there's the matter of the multi-animal household that consists only of cats, and a great many of them. The question arises: How many is too many?

There is no too many if the owners have the resources to deal with a crowd. Like the Simpsons, who have twenty-two cats. They also have a great deal of money, an enormous apartment and six kids who love kitties. Each child has his or her own little coterie of three to four cats, sleeping on their beds at night and changing their groupings according to the whims of the moment. Loyalties shift from time to time and even overnight, but there is neither a cat nor a kid in the remarkable Simpson home who has any doubt about belonging in a circle of warmth and love. I do not mean by this that a houseful of cats necessarily means a houseful of love. For some people, twenty-two cats would be twenty-one too many. Even one cat is one cat too many when there's no individual love and attention.

Which brings me to cat ladies.

They roam the streets of New York and other cities feeding stray cats as lonely and abandoned as themselves. Often they pick up strays and take them to their own rooms or small apartments—or decaying mansions, for all I know—and add them to the crowd they are already sheltering. There, increasing numbers of cats live, eat, breed and die in unhealthy and malodorous quarters.

Mrs. Malkowski was one of my pro bono clients. I imagine every veterinarian in practice has some of these. She was a woman in her sixties who spoke a rather garbled, accented English I could not always grasp completely, but I did understand that she suffered from diabetes and never went to a doctor on her own account. For her cats, yes, but not for herself. Her clothes were little more than rags, and her swollen legs were covered with Ace bandages that were saturated with pus and had a terrible odor.

All I knew about her personally was that she lived in the Bronx and came to my office by subway with two or three cats at a time in a carrier. I could never figure out how she managed the awkward trip, because obviously her legs hurt her, and she walked unsteadily with a cane—which she told me she used not only for support but as a weapon of defense if needed. I could not imagine under what circumstances she would ever have to defend herself, because she obviously had nothing to steal other than a couple of cats and a cane, but the day would come when I was to find out. The ride from her house to my office took probably about an hour or a little more, which I would have thought was agonizing but didn't seem to bother her at all.

When Mrs. Malkowski arrived at our office, we didn't have to see her to know that she was there; we could smell her. She smelled exactly like cat urine, for the most obvious of reasons, and the odor would permeate our usually sweet-smelling offices. We welcomed her, of course, but we always took the cats into an isolated treatment room and kept them there until we were ready to send them home. Most of the diseases they carried were contagious to others, as were the little companions they came with—not just fleas and mites, but larger company.

So when the Malkowski cats arrived, we had to be prepared for instant action as we opened the cat box to examine them, because, invariably, six or seven cockroaches would pop out and start scurrying around. What we did was open the carrier very carefully inside a plastic cloth, yank out the cats, and zap the cockroaches with spray as soon as they scuttled into view.

The cats suffered mainly from upper respiratory infections. I never really knew how many she had, and in fact when I asked her once or twice, she avoided an answer. This, I found, was typical of cat ladies. So was her idea of taking care of cats: feed and water them, put a roof over their heads if you had one and they were willing, and bring them to somebody like me for treatment whenever they got sick enough to capture attention.

I only saw the sick ones, but I doubt if any of them looked good. Mrs. Malkowski's cats were never combed or groomed to any degree. Their fur was scruffy; their eyelids were invariably glued together with pus, and very often there was pus or mucus running out of their noses. Not surprisingly, they were often covered with fleas. All things considered, they were never a pretty sight.

Nor was there ever a time when they could be vaccinated, because as soon as she got a new kitten, it would be exposed to all her other sick cats, and this became a cycle. I'm sure she had a houseful of sick cats perpetually, even though I know I didn't see them all. She used to come to my office about once a month with a different contingent of cats, and I don't recall getting to know any of them. I suspect Mrs. Malkowski had several veterinarians who felt sorry for her or for her cats, and she would take turns going from one to another so as not to take advantage of any one veterinarian—or run the risk of being refused as a pro bono client if she showed up once too often.

I gathered from her that she fed every stray cat she saw in the city, forswearing the more costly commercial product and serving up vintage cat-lady food like Pawline's Mrs. McGonigle: boiled chicken gizzards, rice, barley and vegetables, cooked up in something I envisioned as a witch's cauldron, and basically quite nutritious. She was a brave woman, in her way, or at least a singularly single-minded one. At odd moments, she would tell me where she had found one cat or another, and it was clear that she walked into all sorts of unsavory places— alleyways, junkyards, derelict parks, garbage-strewn empty lots—wherever stray cats were likely to roam. And no doubt the cats would gather for food when they saw her coming.

There came a time when six or seven weeks passed with no sign of Mrs. Malkowski. I began to wonder about this, because I had come to expect her routine monthly visit. Not that I missed her or her cats, but I did think it rather strange that she hadn't appeared.

Three days later, she showed up with her battered cat carrier. I noticed that her dress seemed clean, and the cat odor wasn't nearly as pungent as usual. She also had clean bandages on her legs, and her hair looked almost combed.

I complimented her on her appearance and observed that I'd been wondering why we hadn't seen her lately.

She said, "Oh, Dr. Padwee, I muz tell you what hoppen to me. It was like a, what you say, nightmare."

Mrs. Malkowski proceeded to tell me an extraordinary story. There is no way that I can tell it in her words or attempt her accent, but this is the gist of it:

Reading the *Daily News* on the subway one morning, she noticed an ad for kittens to be given away to a good home. Interested cat lovers should call such and such a number. Mrs. Malkowski needed more cats like cats need more fleas, but she could never resist a kitten. When she got off the train, she went straight to the nearest public telephone, as she had no phone at home, and by some miracle, it was in working order. Not a good time for a miracle, as events would demonstrate.

A very nice woman's voice answered and told her she had twelve young kittens and they were just wonderful, but she couldn't afford to keep them. Her name, she said, was Mrs. Desmond, and if Mrs. Malkowski would care to come over next morning, she would be delighted. Midmorning tea, perhaps?

What a nice lady.

When Mrs. Desmond said, "Come over," Mrs. Malkowski quickly learned, she meant it literally. The nice lady lived deep in the Greenpoint section of Brooklyn, and her visitor needed to come over a bridge to get there. Well, at least it wasn't Queens.

They agreed to meet at the Brooklyn subway station of Mrs. Desmond's choice, as the directions for finding her house were rather complicated, and the next morning Mrs. Malkowski rose early in her Bronx home and undertook the long trip to the other outer borough. What with a wrong train or two, a bad connection and ongoing track work on the bridge, it took Mrs. Malkowski almost three hours by subway to get to the appointed place.

Leaning on her cane, she looked around. The only woman who seemed to be waiting for someone seemed oddly familiar. Mrs. Desmond? . . . Could she possibly have met her somewhere before? The woman started toward her with a less than radiant smile, and as she did so, Mrs. Malkowski saw in her—herself. Not really herself, but an unruly looking woman of indeterminate years wearing ill-fitting old clothes and sporting scratch marks on her hands.

Another cat woman.

"Mrs. Malkowski? You're late. I suppose it was the trains."

She didn't seem to be particularly sympathetic.

Off they went together, taking shortcuts through the backs of gas stations and down alleys until they reached a semi-industrial area near a junkyard, and Mrs. Malkowski was quite bewildered when they stopped at what the woman said was her house. It was dismayingly dilapidated. Obviously it hadn't been painted within anyone's living memory. The roof was in disrepair, the fence was sagging, the grass was overgrown, and the sidewalk was broken. All in all, it was not an inviting scene. It seemed like a place a rather strange person might live in.

She shot an uneasy glance at her hostess as they entered the house.

They were in an unfurnished space just outside the kitchen when Mrs. Malkowski, who had not yet seen a cat in the house but detected the characteristic odor of a sizable cat population, asked: "Where are the kittens?"

Mrs. Desmond yanked at a chain and opened a trapdoor in the floor.

"They're down in the cellar," she said. "Down those steps."

Our heroine didn't like the looks of the steps, but she did want to see the kittens. So she hobbled down with her cane, expecting Mrs. Desmond to join her but not caring much if she didn't. When she reached bottom, the light was dim but she could see that she was standing on a dirt floor littered with indefinable objects, some of which were stationary and some not. Trash! Cats!

Cats were all over the place—scrabbling at the dirt, running around, scrambling up on the pipes and on the furnace, lurking in nooks and crannies, chomping on cat chow, meowing, howling and spitting at each other. It was a rather hellish scene, Mrs. Malkowski thought, or was she thinking of purgatory? There must have been a hundred cats down in that dark basement, which was gradually getting lighter as her eyes became accustomed to it.

Now it was just light enough for her to find her way around. There were open cans of cat food all over the place. Some had dried; some had not. Fecal matter and urine were scattered and splashed about. The stench of decay and excrement was breathtaking. If Mrs. Malkowski thought it was bad, it must have been really bad. There was no kitty litter down there; just old, soiled newspapers and filth. And cats. All shapes, colors and sizes of cats. Little cats, big cats, males, females, all manner of cats.

Mrs. Malkowski decided to come up for a breath of fresh air, and as she started up the stairs, the woman screamed at her. She sounded crazy.

"You love the cats!" she screeched. "Now take care of them! They're your cats! Clean up that basement! And you're not getting upstairs until you do that."

Clean up the basement!

Mrs. Malkowski crept back down the stairs and obediently set to work. She felt sorry for the cats, and she was scared, and she couldn't think what else to do. With whatever cleaning equipment she could find, she set to work to put some order into the disgusting chaos.

Hours later, she said, she climbed back up the stairs and begged for mercy at the open trapdoor, where the woman was waiting. She was starving, but she dared not ask for anything more than just a drink of water and a chance to sit down. The woman agreed to let her come up for a few minutes. Exhausted, she drank the water and then made a sudden dart for the front door.

"Oh, no, you don't!" the woman screamed at her. "You're not finished with your work yet! You stay here!" But Mrs. Malkowski had had enough. She shook her cane at her captor and sidled out through the doorway. The woman seized a heavy frying pan and followed her with it, aiming for the head. Mrs. Malkowski held her off with stabbing motions of the cane until she managed to back through the fence gateway, where she tried to turn, and then the woman let her have it with the frying pan over the head.

Mrs. Malkowski collapsed on the sidewalk. Dimly she realized that a passerby was leaning over to question her, and then she saw the police. Next thing she knew, she was in a hospital emergency room.

She was terrified at being in such a place, but it was a blessing in disguise. The doctors kept her there, and in the hospital they treated her for all her ailments—her diabetes, her swollen and ulcerated legs, her malnutrition and the concussion perpetrated by the cat woman with her frying pan.

Mrs. Malkowski was there for two weeks, a very sick person being cared for after years of self-neglect, and on returning home, she was so weak that she didn't have the strength to go out of the house. When she came to me with a couple of sniveling cats and told me about her incredible experience, she admitted to me that she had far too many cats than she could really handle. And as for that other woman! She rolled her eyes. So many cats! So many sick! Such awful food! So much dirt! She is a crazy person! And with that, Mrs. Malkowski lowered her eyes.

This was a case—I thought, after she had left—where love was blind. She had loved her cats so much that she was blind to the fact that she wasn't really giving them the best of care. And then something incredible had happened to point this out to her.

There were details missing from her story. I wondered where she'd gotten the cleaning equipment to clean up that basement; I wondered who had looked after her cats while she was gone; I wondered how she had obtained food for them when she came back; I wondered about the condition of her own apartment, as I had wondered before. But there were some questions I simply didn't want to ask; answers I didn't really want to know.

And did the episode actually occur? That, I would really like to have known. It seemed like a dream . . . a strange kind of warning dream with a message of sorts. A lesson, a parable, a fable. Of course, I don't believe in that. But something did happen; she actually had changed.

I didn't see her too often after that. She made another couple of visits, and then no more. And I started to wonder if *I* was the one who had dreamed her story.

Yet she is still around the city in various guises. I see them today, women in stained old clothes picking their way through garbage dumps and abandoned lots with their pails of food and battered foil pans, feeding ever-growing numbers of the hungry. And I am torn between admiration and something close to despair.

What they are doing is, I suppose, well-meant and generous, but I can't determine exactly why they do it and what they think they are achieving. Their kindness tends to increase the stray cat population and, ultimately, the destruction of even more homeless animals; and I like to think that, perhaps, Mrs. Malkowski might have caught on to something like that.

I also like to think that she is taking better care of herself.

CHAPTER EIGHT

Responsibilities *for* Pawline

GOOD NEWS!" I ANNOUNCED. Pawline and Nancy Gardner were in my examination room. Nancy had come to me right after Pawline's romantic interlude, worried about the back of the kitty's neck where the stud had bitten her. To Nancy it had looked like a really savage attack.

"Sounds like everything went according to plan," I observed, parting the back of Pawline's ruff. "Here we are . . . a couple of small lesions, nothing serious."

There were also a few nip marks left by the tomcat's embrace, as there often are, and they are truly nothing to worry about. I cleaned the area and applied some antibiotic ointment. "No reason everything shouldn't be just fine," I told Nancy. But if she is pregnant, I'll need to tell you how to take care of her."

"So give me the lecture," Nancy said.

"Let's find out first, why don't we?" I suggested. "I want you to come back in three weeks so that we can make a positive diagnosis of pregnancy. The gestation period in cats is sixty-three days, give or take a day or so. This means that she may not have the kittens exactly on day sixty-three. It could be one or two days before or one or two days after."

"I read you," said Nancy. "I'll make an appointment."

So here we were, three weeks later, and I had just finished palpating the uterus. It was enlarged, as I had expected, and I could confirm that Pawline was definitely pregnant. To make doubly sure, I took an X ray to see what was going on inside the uterus. (Today we would use an ultrasound scan, which gives us a two-dimensional image.) What we could see was not only the embryonic kittens but their size and stage of development. I easily detected three embryos, one a little larger than the others.

"No doubt about it," I told Nancy. "Three on the way, and due in about six weeks."

Nancy was thrilled. At this time in her life, she had no children of her own, and there was something about Pawline having kittens that seemed to strike a chord in her that was more than sentimental. For a fleeting moment, I wondered how bad she would feel if anything were to go wrong, which—let's face it—is always a possibility, but I quickly talked myself out of such thoughts. She had made her choice. Anyway, we had no reason to suppose that anything might go amiss.

We discussed nutrition. Pawline, as one of my regular clients, was already on a completely balanced diet. We would maintain her on this but increase the amount of food a little bit each week and add a vitamin-mineral supplement. And we made a date for her final checkup. Pawline purred like a steam engine and hopped back into her carrier.

When she came in for her checkup at the seventh week of pregnancy, I suggested that we take another X ray to make sure the kittens were in the right position and stage of development.

Nancy was a little dubious. "An X ray now? Couldn't that be harmful at this point?"

"No, no, no. Would I suggest it? No, it won't harm either Pawline or her babies. And I do feel an X ray is indicated at this stage." In fact, I did want to check on the size and positioning of the kittens, which would be helpful to know if any problems should arise during the delivery.

Pawline took the picture session with her usual cheerful equanimity. She herself was in fine shape, and I could see nothing really unusual about the kittens—not much bigger than little mice, at this point— although one had already established itself as top cat. It was definitely bigger than the other two. This is often the case: In most litters, especially those larger than Pawline's, there is one kitten that has a little more edge than the others and one that has a little less. Sometimes it has a lot less, and people unkindly refer to it as the runt of the litter.

We had here three well-positioned kittens developing on schedule, with one apparently taking the lead. Mother, as usual, was doing very well. "This is exciting!" said Nancy. "I want the kittens born at home. I want to see them being born."

"Most household kittens are actually born at home," I observed, "but not necessarily when anyone's watching. So if you really want to see this blessed event, you're going to have to try to dictate the place and then keep an eye on Pawline. I don't think it's going to be all that easy; kitty mothers have minds of their own. But try your best."

In fact, most of my client cats have their kittens at home. Their owners are often quite surprised to find little scrawny cat babies staggering out of the hall closet, not having had a clue about the due date until the happening and only bringing the kittens in afterwards for a checkup and a stern comment by me about being more observant. It's usually the owners of the more exotic and costly breeds who bring their queens into our clinic to give birth or owners who are squeamish or afraid they won't do the right thing when the time comes. These are mostly city dwellers. Certainly, country people tend to think that the cat knows what to do without being told.

I described to Nancy the setup I think is appropriate for a home birth, and though it often doesn't work, I wish it would. Really, doctors don't want their patients wandering around having their babies under the bathroom pipes or on the upper shelf of the linen closet, or their owners wandering around looking for the cats.

"Find a place in the house," I said, "a quiet and secluded place, like your sewing room"—Nancy looked at me like I'd just stepped out of the Middle Ages—"and set it up for Pawline. A large cardboard box will be fine as a whelping pen—that is, a delivery pen. Cut a round hole in the box, about ten inches above the floor, so that Pawline can get in and out and yet the kittens won't be able to leave. Line it with some comfortable old rags, entice her into it and get her used to it, starting now. A few little treats placed in the box might help."

Privately, I thought that Pawline would of course use anything but the prepared place for having her kittens, but one could only try to do the right thing.

I spent about fifteen or twenty minutes explaining all the details of preparation for the birth and what to look for as the kittens came out. Nancy seemed a little daunted, but faced it all with a determined chin.

"And call me any time," I said. "Call me if you change your mind or if there's something you don't like the looks of. She's my favorite kitty, you know that." I stroked Pawline's cheek, and she licked me with her little rough tongue.

I got a quick and cheerful call from Nancy on about day sixty. Pawline had turned paws down on the old cashmere sweater-lined box prepared for her and was scouting a bureau drawer carelessly left open.

Early in the morning of the sixty-third day, Pawline, right on schedule, started to strain in the laundry basket she had elected to plop into. Nancy called her office to take this red-letter day off. Contractions were coming every ten minutes, but nothing else seemed to be happening. Watching and waiting, Nancy got concerned by the lack of action and had me on the telephone for advice with the first little spasm and several times thereafter. Well, I *had* told her to keep in touch. And I had fully expected to hear from her that often, because when kittens are being born to caring owners, there nearly always are last-minute questions and a lot of anxiety on the part of the people.

"Is she straining now?"

"Not really. In fact, she doesn't seem to be doing any work at all."

Pawline was giving out little cries at times, Nancy said, but there were no signs of distress . . . or of kittens, either.

I suggested that she give Pawline a little slack: back off a bit, everybody relax, keep an eye on her from a distance, then call again.

After two hours, she did. Nothing had changed. Mother-to-be was still making small mewing sounds, and contractions were still coming regularly, but they weren't producing anything.

"Bring her in," I said. "Nothing particularly unusual is happening and I don't want you to be alarmed, but I would like to check her."

Pawline arrived regally, in what amounted to a portable lying-in bed: a splendid new cat carrier lined with soft towels to make it more comfortable for her and to absorb some of the discharge from her vulva. I greeted the queen and lifted her to the table.

Everything seemed to be normal and Pawline herself in fine condition, but the uterus was not contracting strongly enough to push out the kittens. This is called uterine inertia, and it is not uncommon. Meanwhile, the kittens were still well-positioned and ready to be pushed. I was going to have to give them a nudge.

"Oxytocin," I told my technician.

He nodded briefly; brought me what I'd asked for.

Nancy raised inquiring eyebrows.

"Oxytocin," I repeated. "It's a pituitary extract. It'll increase the strength of the contractions. A painless and safe injection. Okay?"

We gave Pawline the injection and put her in our intensive care unit, where we kept her under constant observation. In a few minutes, she was pushing vigorously.

"All right, here we go!" Moments later, her firstborn appeared: a very large, healthy female kitten. I took the kitten from the mother and rubbed her between two towels to stimulate her respiration. She gave a few little mewling cries, and it was obvious at once that she was breathing easily.

"My goodness, she's kind of ugly, actually," said Nancy.

"It's all that damp and sticky hair," I replied.

We wiped off all the discharge from the afterbirth, then I put a pair of forceps on the umbilical cord, cut the cord and tied it. She was a fine specimen, as upfront and bossy as I had thought this big kitten would be. I gave her back to Pawline, who nuzzled her. Kitty Number One staggered right over to nurse, which she did with lip-smacking enjoyment as if she'd come a long way for this and knew just what to do. By this time Nancy was captivated. "Ooohhh," she murmured. "Aaahhh!"

The next kitten arrived some minutes later without further need of injection. It was, as I'd thought, much smaller than the first. Kitty Number Two, a little male, also knew where to go and what to do, but he was having some difficulty in doing it. Milk was running from his nostrils.

I picked him up, pried open his tiny mouth, and looked at the area of the hard palate very closely. This area separates the nasal cavity from the oral cavity. I dried it with a cotton swab in order to get a clear look at the tissue. I reached for my binocular magnifying glasses; with them, I could see a small opening in the hard palate. This is commonly known as a cleft palate. When a kitten with this condition nurses, some or most or occasionally all of the milk seeps through the opening into the nasal cavity and out the nostrils.

"What is it?" Nancy said anxiously. "What's wrong?"

"He's a sloppy eater," I said. "But he'll be fine." I returned him to the feeding station.

And, indeed, this kitty's situation could have been far worse. He was an energetic little chap who kept on trying even though it wasn't easy. The good news was that the opening, though abnormal, was so small that I felt it would fuse without treatment within a short time. I'd seen this condition many times before, and the palate generally closes by itself. Until that time, this little fellow would be able to feed without too much difficulty, sloshing and snorting his milk but getting more than enough to keep him going. Or so I believed.

The third kitten emerged. It was another male, small indeed, and very weak, an undersized little mite about the length of my forefinger. Pawline gave it a little cuff in the right direction, but even then, it had difficulty finding a teat to suckle. Unlike his brother, who was doing a good job of getting his mother's milk despite the droplets that ran out of his nose, this tiny tyke seemed to have no energy at all. I made a fast surface check of all the things we usually look at in the newborn—tail, legs, crawl reflexes, anus, genitalia, thoracic cage, abdomen, remnants of umbilical cord, skin, head, neck, skull, ears, eyes, mouth—and all externals were fine. So was the inside of the mouth. But Kitty Number Three wasn't suckling. Even when we held him at the nipple, he wouldn't nurse.

"Oh, I can't bear it," Nancy said faintly.

I sighed.

He was a very weak little cat. There was no visible deformity; nothing obvious to tell me why this was so; but so it was.

My technician murmured, "Fading kitten syndrome."

"Which means? . . . " Nancy looked bewildered.

Fading kitten syndrome is the sort of name that means almost whatever you want it to mean as applied to a nonthriving newborn cat. As a manifestation, it has many causes and many aspects. We use the term for kittens that are born in a very weak condition, cause unknown, and who die directly after birth or within a week or two. It also describes the fate of kittens that seem healthy at birth but die ten to twelve weeks later after getting weaker and weaker and simply fading away.

Whatever the cause of whatever the symptom, the problem is generally acquired in utero. Some common causes are infectious diseases or parasites, and I saw no signs of these in Pawline. Others could be medication given to the pregnant cat, which we knew was not the case, or poor nutrition during pregnancy, again not a factor with Pawline. And then there are congenital abnormalities. We knew a lot about Pawline, but we didn't know about the latter; we didn't know what was in her genes. Even a bouncing, healthy cat can harbor defective genes to the detriment of her offspring. This happens with humans, and it happens with cats as well.

The little chap was not going to make it, I told Nancy.

"Can't you save him?" she pleaded.

I shook my head. All indications were that this kitten had acute congestive cardiomyopathy. He was breathing with great difficulty and becoming cyanotic—I could see the bluish cast of his tongue and mucous membranes—and I knew he would die within a few hours. In these cases, the thin-walled heart is hugely dilated and the muscle fiber is degenerative. I was almost certain that the lungs and thoracic cavities were filled with fluid. There was no way we could have predicted this abnormality or detected it beforehand.

"No, I can't save him," I said. "If I were to employ all possible life-saving measures, you would be bankrupt in about ten minutes and he still wouldn't survive. Let's not have him suffer, Nancy. It's best to let him go now."

And so we did.

The saddest fact here was that Nancy was the loser, not Pawline, who was contentedly nursing her big, vigorous baby and the milky-nosed little struggler. Cats can't count. Pawline didn't even know that one of her kittens was missing. I've delivered thousands and thousands of kittens, a few defective but most of them beautiful, and much as I truly love cats, the truth of the matter is that too many kittens are being born every day. Always plenty more where these come from . . . as many as the millions that live.

Nancy took the mother and her two babies home. For the little fellow, the outcome was just as I'd hoped. By four weeks of age, the hard palate was perfectly healed: no more cleft palate, no more splashing through the nose. He'd never be as big as his sister, but he was normal and happy.

Nancy had decided to call the female Sassy because of her obvious feistiness, and the little guy, Little Guy. Pawline, as robust as ever, looked very pleased with herself as she nursed her babies, but she was already getting back her wanderlust for forbidden places and back-yard fences. She divided her time between getting trapped in the washing machine, jumping into the dryer, chattering at blue jays, training her kittens and watching a little television. A rich, full life it was, with no great emphasis on becoming the ideal mother.

For the kittens, we started supplementary feeding at five weeks: a little milk, then some scraped beef and a dab of baby food. At six weeks, nursing was over and the kittens fed themselves, which they did with healthy gusto. At seven weeks, Nancy gave them away. Her brother wanted Little Guy, whom he renamed Chester, and her sister adopted Sassy. The Gardners wanted only one cat, their adored Pawline, but they wanted to keep her kids in the family. Nancy phoned me with the adoption news, and I was pleased. Now three families would be happy.

A month or so later, all Pawline's milk had dried up and we were able to spay and declaw her at the same time. Her maternal responsibilities, never a big thing with her, were over. And, as usual, she was totally unfazed.

Nancy called to bring me up to date on the adoptees and relay the latest Pawline bulletin. And report other news as well:

"I guess Pawline was something of an inspiration to John and me," she said a little breathlessly, "not that she's such a great role model. But I want you to know—we're going to have a baby! And Pawline can help to bring the Gardner baby up. Or all of them, if that turns out to be the case."

Well, that was just lovely, and I said so. But there was also a little touch of irony here. Nancy had wanted Pawline to have kittens so that she herself could contemplate the miracle of birth and the adorable sight of a mother cat nursing the kittens. But the wonder of it all was lost on Pawline, and now Nancy was going to do it herself. With, one hoped, a human child.

What a *nice* ending, I thought.

CHAPTER NINE

The Bleeding New Year's Eve Cat

N EITHER THE HENDERSONS NOR I had planned to spend one of the most festive nights of the year with blood dripping from our hands, while the rest of the town made resolutions and washed them down with champagne, but their New Year's Eve party ended early, and most of mine took place on the telephone.

What happened was that Skippy was in very serious trouble. I was already out on the town, celebrating with some friends in their East Side Manhattan home, when I got the beep on the brand-new beeper my wife had given me for Christmas. Nothing would induce me to use one of those things anymore, but this was before the beeper epidemic had spread to every doctor, lawyer, drug dealer and hip-hop artist in the city of New York, and I felt quite important when my new toy signaled a telephone alert.

I called the given number, a vaguely familiar one.

I should explain that my wife and I were only in the city for that one night. We were commuters at this time, having recently bought a house about an hour's train and subway ride from my clinic in midtown Manhattan, and our arrangement for New Year's Eve was to stay overnight with our party hosts in their apartment in the East nineties. It was thus by chance that the clinic was only a cab ride away.

Dick Henderson picked up my call, sounding agitated to the point of hysteria and full of apologies for dragging me away from a party. Their cat, Skippy, was on the point of death. He and his wife, Henderson said, had left their New Year's Eve party early because his wife hadn't been feeling well, and when they got home, the living room was in such a mess that they thought there must have been a wounded intruder or a cat fight or some sort of terrible accident. The cat was lying semi-comatose in a pool of blood, and there was blood splashed on the furniture, but the curious part was that there was no other damage in the apartment and no sign of a break-in. And of course Skippy couldn't have gotten into a fight because there were no other animals in the place, so he must have slashed himself on something, but they saw nothing—

I cut this short. Mrs. H. was making urgent, despairing sounds in the background, and the cat wasn't getting any better while Dick talked. I said: "Wrap him in a blanket, put him in his carrier and get him to my office. You have a hot water bottle? Put that in with him. Meet me at the clinic in fifteen minutes."

And this on New Year's Eve! But Skippy and his owners were clients of long standing. Besides, Mrs. Henderson was a semi-invalid and particularly devoted to the rotund Skippy. She would be devastated if she lost him. I ignored my wife's resigned look and called my night technician to explain what was happening and alert him to expect a bloody cat and one or two very distressed people. There is always someone on the clinic premises at night, not so much for emergencies as to monitor the hospitalized animals and keep them comfortable, so I knew we'd be ready for action.

Tony, my technician, was waiting for me.

Both Hendersons, still in evening clothes, arrived with the cat. Dick had taken Skippy out of his carrier and was holding him against a tuxedo shirt that was covered with fresh blood. "I told Annie she shouldn't come," he said, "but she wanted to be with the cat." Annie Henderson looked ashen. It was clear that she would have been better off at home in bed. Skippy, ordinarily a cheerful orange cat, looked as truly awful as only a very sick cat can look. Yet he obviously wasn't undernourished. In fact, he had put on quite a bit of padding in the months since I'd last seen him, and he'd been chubby enough then.

But this I noticed only peripherally at first. My urgent concern was to find the source of the blood and determine what kind of accident could possibly have caused it.

I stretched the cat out on the examination table. He was as unresisting as a beanbag and about as cooperative. His eyes flickered open very briefly, just long enough for me to see that they were as dull and leaden as his body. He was one miserable kitty, but it was immediately apparent that he had not been in any kind of accident—unless it was something totally freakish that I'd never encountered before.

There was no external wound. None.

An internal hemorrhage, then, probably urinary. Not altogether surprising in an overweight cat. I checked temperature, pulse and respiration: all systems low. Running my hands over the abdomen, I palpated the bladder. It was the size of a softball, and very taut. Aha! I said to myself; and at that moment, the cat produced a little squirt of urine that looked like one hundred percent blood.

Dick stepped back and said, "There!" as if I had doubted the blood on his shirt. "I see that," I said mildly. "This cat has not impaled itself on the kitchen carving knife. This cat is suffering from what we call urethral block."

"Meaning what?"

"Meaning that the urethra is obstructed and the cat can't urinate. What's happened is that the pressure of the urine not being able to leave the bladder has caused a rupture of the blood vessels of the bladder wall. It probably began as cystitis, which we think is due to a bacterial infection. In effect, it's severe inflammation of the bladder. That's where all the blood has been coming from."

"*That much?*"

"Yes, well, big cat, big bladder, bad rupture. The blood loss is serious and so is the obstruction. Let's see . . . how old is Skippy?" I glanced at his chart. "Going on six. That's about the right age for a fat cat to have this kind of trouble." I skewered Dick with a look, because I'd warned him before about a possible obesity problem with Skippy, but it wasn't lecture time yet. This was a near-critical situation that had to be handled at once.

"Okay, first thing we have to do, we have to unblock the cat—get rid of the obstruction in the urethra—and then remove the urine from the bladder. There's no sense either of you waiting around. We have a lot to do, and it'll be a while before we get much response from Skippy. So you and Annie had best go home. I'll be in touch."

That was all right with Dick, but Annie didn't want to leave the cat in the hospital.

"Why can't I wait?" she wanted to know. "Can't you just give him something and let us take him home?"

"It's a little more complicated than that," I said carefully, not wanting to alarm her further. There was a possibility that Skippy might not make it through the night, even in the hospital and almost certainly not at home. This was not a situation where you could say, "Take a tablet and go to sleep—oh, yes, and give the cat one, too—and bring him in first thing in the morning." This was intensive-care time. "He's going to need certain procedures that we have to do here, and we need to watch him to see how he responds. Tony?"

Tony handed me a filled syringe. "This is a sedative," I explained, administering a quick shot under the skin. "Skippy's in pain, and we have to alleviate that first. Then we'll have to relieve the pressure on the bladder and get him onto medication. So you see, he really needs to be here."

They fussed a little and made me promise I'd call at any hour if there was anything to report.

I promised. They fussed some more, but I chased them out; I think they left with some relief.

As soon as the cat was comfortably under sedation, we moved him to the treatment room, where we arranged him on a table and gently tied him into place to enable us to attach the tubes. Then we put him on intravenous antibiotics and fluid therapy for shock and dehydration. Tony prepared to take an X ray, and I made a phone call to my wife at the party. "I'll be a while," I said, hearing sounds of festivity in the background, and I told her what was happening. She said, "Fine, keep in touch," and went back to join the fun. "Save some for me," I muttered, hanging up.

The truth is, I was perfectly happy where I was.

I went back to Skippy and palpated his swollen bladder again. I had no doubt about the nature of his problem. What I didn't know was how severe it might prove to be.

This cat was suffering from FUS—feline urologic syndrome—a term for urinary obstruction in male cats. Unfortunately it is not an uncommon disease; it is, however, extremely distressing for all concerned, particularly the cat. Cats with FUS are unable to pass their urine because of deposits of minute crystals or sandy sludge or sometimes plugs of mucus in the urinary canal, usually near the exit. What we call gravel, or a buildup of crystalline material, is quite often found, and this is usually not too difficult to flush out with a catheter if we get to it promptly. There might, on the other hand, be a concentration of stones, which is something else again. If this cat had developed stones, we would need to operate as soon as he could stand the surgery. But, with any luck, we could manage with the catheter.

Whatever the case, this was genuinely an emergency situation. Without early treatment, the cat would surely die.

The X ray of Skippy's bladder showed gravel in the urethra, more than enough to block the passage of the urine and build up enormous pressure within the bladder and against the bladder wall. But at least he didn't have stones. I was relieved; he looked far too weak for surgery. We inserted a catheter to draw off the bladder contents and reduce the pressure, sewing the device into place so that the cat wouldn't dislodge it when he started to move—*if* he started to move. The urine coming out looked like pure blood, and the bladder was still as round and firm as a ball. Skippy was losing a lot of blood, but we were pumping fluids back into him as fast as we could, and all we could do now was watch and wait.

He lay as if dying, not moving, not changing, not caring. The catheter drained slowly and silently into a pail beneath the table. I told Tony to catch up on some sleep. It looked as though I'd be around for a while. He made a quick check on the animals in the recovery room next door and went off to the apartment upstairs.

I sat on the high chair near my patient and wrote up my report, looking at Skippy and noting the almost imperceptible rise and fall of his overpadded rib cage. I checked his pulse again on the large artery of the hind leg and took a swab of the urine to make a culture. I went back to my chair and wondered about a lot of things, starting with, Why and how had this cat been permitted to get so fat? Obesity predisposes animals to any number of disorders, and in the male cat, FUS is high on the list. And yet the precise cause of the condition is not yet known. Dietary imbalance could be one factor. If a cat eats only dry food or doesn't drink enough water, the salts in the urine may become concentrated and form deposits that block the urinary canal, generally near the end of the penis. A diet unusually high in magnesium or ash may produce an alkaline urine, which can also lead to obstruction. In Skippy's case, it looked as though his diet was unusually high in food.

For a fleeting moment, I felt there was something ironic about my spending New Year's Eve thinking about cat urine, but I let that thought go because, as a matter of simple fact, I often think about cat urine. It's a big thing in the world of cats, and quite often in the lives of cat owners. Any undue display of it, such as incontinence or its appearance on a new rug or spraying to mark territory, may be as revealing as it is maddening. I once had a patient named Splash, a middle-aged guy who strayed in from the cold and inserted himself into a household that already included three cats. His particular trick was to back up against his new owners' legs and let go with a brisk stream of ill-smelling cat graffiti. For some reason, his new owners didn't care for this and brought the cat to see me. There was nothing wrong with the fellow that neutering and extra doses of affection couldn't fix; all he was saying was that he was there to stay and that everything and everyone in that household was *his*.

Now, as for Skippy: Why should this cat have FUS? The problem occurs in all breeds and at all ages, to neutered and unneutered cats, to indoor and outdoor cats and cats fed on any kind of food. Usually a common factor is that the cat doesn't drink enough water, which is not something a cat owner can do much about other than leaving bowls of fresh water at strategic places around the house and serving up food with considerable moisture in it. And that isn't always enough.

A further question: Why hadn't Dick and Annie noticed anything wrong with the cat until it was almost at the point of bursting? This isn't something that happens overnight. There are usually a number of warning signs. In early stages, the cat might be either listless or restless and irritable. It makes frequent trips to the litter pan and strains uncomfortably once there. Sometimes it gives little cries of pain and leaves its litter pan to urinate somewhere else around the house, and an alert owner might note that its abdomen is enlarged and tender. In advanced cases, the cat might strain and cry almost constantly, vomiting when it isn't drooling and crawling into dark places to hide. Yet Skippy had exhibited no such glaringly obvious signs of anguish.

Well, it was puzzling. He must have shown some symptoms, but perhaps his people had been too consumed with their own concerns to notice his discomfort. That, I thought, must surely be it. With problems of their own, it simply hadn't occurred to them that the cat wasn't his usual playful self.

A puppy whimpered, and I stopped thinking about Skippy for a moment. Little animal sounds whispered in the recovery room next door. It was like a tiny jungle in there, a world apart that made me feel completely isolated from the city around me. The place always affected me that way at night, although as my practice had grown and I'd added assistants to my staff, I hadn't spent a great deal of time there after regular office hours. The most memorable occasion had been a winter blackout in New York City back in the 'seventies, when the lights had gone out at about six P.M. just as I was doing a cesarean section on, of all things, a fifty-pound boa constrictor.

As soon as I could afford to do so, I had set up my animal hospital on a round-the-clock basis. There was always a veterinarian living in an apartment overhead. I wanted a qualified practitioner to be on hand at all times, less for midnight calls, which were few—than to monitor animals recovering from surgery and to medicate those that needed medication. At the same time, we were ready for any surprises. Our supply room was crammed with packaged foods from dog biscuits to bird seed, and our medical cabinets with medical and surgical supplies for man and beast alike. We also, though we didn't have our own generator, had emergency lighting in the form of freestanding flashlights with high-powered beams.

And so, when the lights went out all over the city, we turned on those beams and finished the surgery successfully. I remember an oddity: Just as I was closing the incision, I heard a strangely incongruous sound from the intensive-care room behind me. It was the plaintive baa-ing of a baby goat, alone in very unlikely surroundings on the blackest night of the New York year.

Now I heard the scuttling of tiny feet in the recovery room. The house mouse, I thought absently, and then remembered Leroy the rat. Pitter-patter, he scampered, pitter-patter across the floor of his kennel. He had had a cyst removed from his side and was clearly feeling better. A bird squawked, a little dog yapped, and something rattled the bars of its cage.

Skippy was draining in, draining out, his condition apparently unchanged. I reached for the phone and called my wife at the party. "Nothing new," I said. "Don't hold your breath."

"What're his chances?" she asked. "Fifty-fifty? Everybody wants to know."

"About even. Maybe slightly better."

"Well, good. I'm rooting for him. We're placing bets here. Excitement is running high."

"That's shocking," I said reprovingly. "Very callous. Put five bucks on for me."

I put the phone down and thought about calling the Hendersons. Then I thought not. There was still nothing to say.

On the other hand, at this moment there did seem to be just the slightest change in Skippy's breathing. That little rise and fall of the chest seemed marginally deeper and more regular. I lifted an eyelid, and then a lip, to check for signs of anemia.

I was mildly encouraged by what I saw, but only just enough to get up and stretch for a moment. Checking the flow in the tubes once more, I wandered into the recovery room. In the dim light, I could see Leroy doing laps in his cage, stopping to look up at me and sniff. His owner—she likes to be called his caregiver—was a psychiatrist in a research facility when she came to know Leroy, who at that time was an experimental laboratory rat. She is now in private practice, and Leroy has been with her for three years.

Separated from Leroy by an empty cage was a somnolent Siamese still too groggy from a late-afternoon anesthetic to do anything but give me a baleful, shuttered look. Next, after a couple more empty cages, was the little dog with the plaintive yap, a toy Fox Terrier recovering from a mammary tumor. We exchanged greetings, and I moved on to the next dog cage. Here was Gregor the Brussels Griffon, a stubby-faced little bruiser of a dog who had come in with a hematoma, or blood blister, of the ear.

Squawks of indignation assailed me from overhead. No need for parakeets to be placed on stands, but I rather like them that way. Tarzan and Jane were a pair. Jane was the one with her wing in a sling, metaphorically speaking. It was she who had required hospitalization for the surgical removal of the tumor on her wing; Tarzan had been brought along to keep her company. They both seemed to be in good voice and fine fettle.

Now for the cage-rattler. He was a sweet-faced monkey named Harold, who had come in with a fractured femur and now had a stainless steel pin in his leg. He chattered at me. I said, "Hush, Harold," and he hushed.

That was it. End of rounds.

This was the longest, thirstiest New Year's Eve I'd ever known. In fact, it was well past two o'clock in the morning of New Year's Day, and here I was talking to a monkey.

I was back in the treatment room when the phone rang. Skippy's eyes flickered open.

"What's new?" said my wife the gambler.

"I think the odds may be looking a little better for us," I said cautiously. "But maybe you shouldn't wait up."

"Of course we will. Seriously, how is he?"

"Well, his eyes are wide open at this moment, and they seem to be clearing. But that's not definitive, of course."

We exchanged no-news for a few moments, during which time I learned that the whole party was anxious about the cat and I was interrupted by call-waiting.

"I'm sorry, Dick, not yet," I said. "Maybe soon. I'll call you."

And I was struck, not for the first time in my life, by the casualness with which some people treat their animals' health on an everyday basis and their near-panic in a life-threatening situation. What does it take to get them to notice abnormal behavior in a supposedly beloved pet?

Skippy closed his eyes again.

Ten minutes later, he opened them and raised his head. I stroked it and tickled him lightly about the chin and ears. He began to purr very softly, in short bursts at first and then in a steady rhythm. It was a serene, feathery little sound, not like the anxious, grating purr of a cat that is distressed or in pain. He actually looked quite comfortable and contented.

Half an hour later, I called the Hendersons and told them that Skippy was going to be all right. As for myself, I was going to the remnants of a party, as soon as I'd gotten Skippy moved to an intensive-care cage and aroused Tony to keep watching him. At shortly after three o'clock, I was on my way.

This, basically, is the story of the Bleeding New Year's Eve cat, as my friends and the Hendersons subsequently referred to him. Skippy turned the corner that morning, although we had to keep him in the hospital for another three days, and when his owners came to pick him up, we made a plan for him. First off, they had to recognize that he was not just adorably round but positively obese. He had a fat buildup around the bladder, which made him sluggish, which made him fatter, which in turn made him vulnerable to a lot of diseases. He would have to be put on a low-magnesium, low-calorie diet, and he would have to be made to exercise. We discussed toys for him to chase and climb. Also, he had to be on medication for several weeks to keep his urine at the correct acidity. He had to be kept out of drafts and off cold floors so long as his bladder was weak and inflamed, since cold conditions might predispose him to another attack.

He should be made to drink more water. One way to do this was to add a little salt to his food, which would make him thirsty. Another was to add beef bouillon to his water supply, not only to give him extra salt but also to make the water taste a bit like gravy, which cats usually love. After a while, we would have to decrease the sodium intake, or we would find ourselves with other problems. Finally: keep his litter box clean, and inspect it every day for the minutest trace of blood.

And call me any time, but let me see him again in five days.

It was, I think, a happy New Year for all. Annie Henderson had been sure that Skippy would bleed to death, and he had survived. She was so relieved that she felt enormously better. People at the party cheered the cat and toasted me. Several won bets. Those who did not were happy anyway.

Skippy made an uneventful recovery and was fine thereafter. Some cats have a recurrence within a few months, but he did not.

And for a long time to come I had people calling with a pet problem and saying I had been recommended by Skippy's parents.

"You know, the Bleeding New Year's Eve cat."

CHAPTER TEN

CATS 911,

or

The Doctor's Ten Commandments

MORE FAT CATS! I had a week of them not long ago. It was a late Friday afternoon in June. Our last patient was Alice, a beautiful Blue-point Siamese belonging to Amanda Ryan. We hadn't been expecting to see her until fall, even though she had a little weight problem I liked to keep track of.

Ms. Ryan had called barely half an hour before, explaining that she had been planning to go to the Hamptons for the weekend and take Alice with her, but now she didn't think she ought to go—with or without her cat.

P.W. was intrigued. P.W. was one of our two receptionists at the time; both were named Phyllis, which got a little confusing sometimes, so one of the Phyllises had settled for using her initials. The reason P.W. was intrigued was that it wasn't like Amanda Ryan to let anything come between her and her weekend plans, even though she doted on Alice.

"Why, what's the problem?" she asked.

"It's Alice," said Ms. Ryan. "When I came home from work, I saw that Alice hadn't touched her food or even her water. And that is really unusual. Especially the food."

P.W. nodded silently. Alice was always a good eater. In fact, too good an eater.

"But it's our weekend routine to go to the Hamptons in the summer," Amanda went on, sounding somewhat aggrieved, "and I didn't want to change it just because for once she hadn't eaten. But then I picked her up to put her into her carrying cage, and I felt this large swelling in the area of her neck. And it feels warm to the touch. Is there any chance of an appointment?"

"I think this is a CATS 911 emergency," P.W. said gravely. "I would say forget about the Hamptons for now and bring her in right away."

P.W. was very familiar with my Ten Commandments, a little list of the conditions we regard as emergencies. An acute swelling is high on that list, and I think Amanda Ryan must have realized that because most of our clients have a copy of the Big Ten bearing our emergency twenty-four-hour number: CATS 911. She hadn't used it, but she would have been entitled. Other situations warranting instant action are: the cat is bleeding, choking, appears to have ingested poison, has difficulty breathing, is having seizures or convulsions, has had an electric shock, has been struck by a car (usually a hit-and-run)—has fallen from a window, or strains while attempting to urinate.

Most of these problems are immediate attention-getters, but a swelling under the fur is not always readily noticed and may be serious trouble in the form of a cancerous tumor.

The door buzzer buzzed, and in came Amanda with Alice.

I put Alice on the table and stroked her body. There really was a lot of it. Not to mince words, Alice had grown from chubby to obese. Come to think of it, Ms. Ryan was no sylph herself—and that, in fact, was not totally irrelevant to Alice's case.

"On her neck," urged Ms. Ryan. "There!"

"I have it," I said. I palpated a swelling in the upper part of the neck. It was hot to the touch, and fluctuating—pulsing. Not a tumor, I thought. Probably an abscess; it certainly felt like an abscess. I opened Alice's mouth and peered in.

Under her tongue, far back and barely visible, was something that looked like a black dot. I had seen this kind of thing before, and I knew by looking at it that there was a good possibility it would turn out to be the tip of a piece of thread. And in all probability, somewhere in the area there would be a needle attached to it.

Time for an X ray.

In the X ray, the needle showed up like a beacon, lodged in the deep tissues of the pharynx. Here was the root of the abscess, the definitive cause. Alice had swallowed a needle and thread. The needle had migrated to her pharynx with the thread attached to it, and so now we had a nasty infection that would have gotten nastier if Ms. Ryan had been less observant.

Ms. Ryan looked on and gasped.

"But that looks like a needle!" she said.

"Indeed it does," I agreed. "Cats' favorite foreign body. Have any idea how this could have happened?"

"No, I can't think—oh, wait! I guess I do. I was doing some sewing about four or five days ago, making a patchwork quilt for Alice's bed." She shot a rather accusatory look at her cat. "And I suppose I must have left a needle lying around."

"Well, it happens often," I said. "But I've seen worse results than this. Nevertheless, Alice needs surgery. That's the only way we'll be able to get it out, and I'd like to get on with it right now. There's just one thing we have to bear in mind. She'll need a general anesthetic. And she is, as you know, a rather fat kitty, and anesthesia in an obese animal may be slightly risky. But we'll proceed with all possible care."

"I know you will," said Ms. Ryan, looking not at me but at her cat. "Shall I wait for her?"

"Tell you what," I said. "You go home and wait there. I'll call you when it's over and we know that Alice is out of danger. Then you might as well go off for the rest of your weekend."

She left. My tech Tony and I got down to business. We did a thorough pre-operative examination, drawing blood to be tested in our lab for any abnormalities but with particular emphasis on thyroid function; and we put her on the baby scale to weigh her.

"Seventeen pounds," said Tony. "Almost too big for the baby scale. Put her on the platform scale next time."

We use the platform scale for large dogs.

"Not a chance," I said. "Next time we weigh her, she's got to be less than this."

Seventeen pounds. The normal weight for Alice's breed and size is about nine and a half pounds, so she was almost one hundred percent overweight. Her blood test came back normal. There was no clinical reason for her obesity. Alice wasn't a cat, she was a pig. Or chowhound, as we say in the clinic. Here was a case of plain obesity, caused by overeating and lack of exercise.

That settled, we carefully put her under. First, we drained the abscess and flushed it out with an antiseptic solution. Then we traced the needle by following the track of the thread to the needle's eye. Here we were really lucky, because even though we had an X ray and knew approximately where the needle was located, it would have taken much longer to find it if the thread had been broken. But it was intact, it was attached, and it was ours.

We took a pair of forceps and nipped it right out.

Then we put a drain in the incision, kept an eye on the recovering Alice, and called Amanda. She could go off on her weekend now; everything was fine. Call us Monday, we told her. And she did. Alice was on antibiotics and making a very satisfactory recovery. Ms. Ryan had had a nice weekend, but she had worried a lot.

When she took Alice home, I asked her to bring the cat back in five days for a checkup and a little discussion on how to handle Alice's obesity problem. I wasn't looking forward to talking about this with Ms. Ryan, because she was well on the way to obesity herself, and I felt I had to be very tactful in dealing with what might be a touchy subject. This is not a rare predicament: When I see an obese cat in my practice, nine times out of ten, his owner is also fat. The overeater overfeeds the cat. Because of his own appetite, he doesn't realize that the cat is overeating.

Time after time, I have looked from a roly-poly cat to a roly-poly owner—I do this very discreetly, of course—and see a connection. This is not good. The majority of cats eat only to live, although obviously some pleasure principle is involved, and they are not naturally greedy. But something like ten per cent of cats devote their lives to their food and you simply cannot satisfy them. Eating becomes a hobby, *the* hobby, a way of life. They're encouraged by being fed too much, and the result is, they're always hungry, they're always ready to eat, and they are *fat*.

This much I can tell the cat's owner: Obesity shortens the lifetime of an animal and must be tackled as a medical problem. What I can't say is: Obesity shortens the lifetime of a person as well.

But some people catch on.

Alice looked fine when she came back, all seventeen pounds of her. The incision had healed beautifully, and she was looking very pleased with life. The less gratifying news was that she hadn't missed a meal.

"Very nice, Alice," I said, "but it's time to cut back on the calories." I pulled a leaflet from a folder and gave it to Ms. Ryan. "This is Alice's prescription. It's a homemade diet I've been using on cats for about ten years, with occasional variations. You'll find it low in calories but high in volume so that Alice won't feel hungry. Not when she gets used to it, that is. But you must be prepared for a little recalcitrance on her part."

Alice, completely relaxed, yawned and scratched while her owner and I went over the diet together.

"It's a completely balanced diet," I said, "although she may not think so at first. As you see, in its basic form, it consists of cooked chicken, green beans, low-fat cottage cheese and cantaloupe. You're going to want one and a half ounces of boiled, skinless chicken, six ounces of green beans, two ounces of low-fat cottage cheese and two ounces of cantaloupe—which cats generally love. Chop everything up and mix it with the cottage cheese. But if Alice is picky, you can separate the elements. And if she doesn't like beans, which some cats don't, you can substitute canned white asparagus tips, chopped cooked carrots or broccoli, canned mushrooms or chopped spinach. Don't mush this together; just serve it chopped. Sometimes you might want to try boiled beef instead of chicken. Give Alice three or four small feedings a day, plus a vitamin-mineral supplement including taurine—which I will give you, in powder form if you want to mix it with the food, or in pills if you find that easier. This is a very high volume diet, so the cat is never hungry."

"Sounds almost good enough to eat," said Ms. Ryan, "except for that taurine stuff, whatever it is."

"It's a cat thing," I explained. "The only problem we might have is getting Alice to go for this change of diet. We know from past experience that cats don't like to change their eating patterns, especially if the change involves foods they're unfamiliar with."

I knew what we would have to do, but even as I spoke, a thought flashed through my mind: "Why don't *you* try it, Ms. Ryan—set the cat a good example." Naturally, being my tactful self, I wouldn't dream of actually saying anything like that.

"I think I'll try it," said Ms. Ryan. I nearly dropped my stethoscope. "Alice and I will eat the same food for a while. I'd like to lose a few pounds myself. But I'll pass on the cat vitamins."

Feeling quite pleased with all of us, I revealed my plan.

In spite of Alice being a chowhound who loved to eat, changing her diet would be no picnic. She was accustomed to stick-to-the-ribs meals, and we would have to get her used to her new reducing diet by one wile or another. Cats can be very capricious about their food. They can eat the same diet day in and day out and like it. Then, suddenly, they'll turn up their noses at something that's been nectar and ambrosia to them for weeks and demand something entirely different. What that may be is up to you to figure out. But if *you* change the diet abruptly without being asked, they'll refuse the food you're trying to foist off on them—refuse to eat anything at all. So you have to be a little crafty about tapering off the old and sneaking in the new.

Which was what we were about to try to do.

We would start Alice on her new regime with small quantities of the diet food, just a tiny bit at first, mixed in with the old, accustomed foods. As the days went by, we would gradually increase the new and decrease the old until we got onto the completely new diet. This would take about two to three weeks, I thought, by which time she should not only be on the reducing diet but actually liking it. And if Ms. Ryan was serious about dieting herself and refrained from filling her kitchen with tempting odors of baking fish and broiling steak, Alice might find it a little easier to adjust.

"Well, good luck and enjoy your meals," I said to Amanda and Alice. "See you next week."

I spent the next few days dealing with cat problems that required close attention—matters of prolonged appetite loss, repeated throwing up, constant dry coat, continued listlessness or apathy, diarrhea, sensitivity to touch, and subtle changes in mood or disposition. Something has to be done about these cases, and without unreasonable delay, but they don't merit CATS 911 calls. Often, they don't merit a call at all. There are times not to panic, times to stop and think, and the devoted cat owner will understand this: Waco is vomiting hairballs, not his guts. Chloe hasn't lost her appetite, she just doesn't care for the peas and carrots in her Primavera Stew. Quark sleeps eighteen hours a day, because that is what cats do best. Mao Mao is apparently constipated and hasn't stirred from his perch on a kitchen shelf for two days. His owner the restaurateur is really worried . . .

This, in fact, was a case that did require some hurry-up attention. It involved my next fat cat.

Mr. Wong was the owner of a large Chinese restaurant in the suburbs, not too far from where I lived at the time. It was a Sunday afternoon when he called me at home and told me that my friend Ellsworth Smith, one of his regular customers and a cat lover, had given him my name and number. I knew that Smith ate at his place at least once a week and loved the food. I told him this, and Mr. Wong was pleased, but he sounded distraught and sad. In fact, I thought he might even be crying. His pet cat, he said, the one who lived in the restaurant, had been sick for four or five days, and for the last couple of days, he been just lying on his favorite shelf in the kitchen, not moving, scarcely breathing. Mr. Wong feared that he was dying. He begged me to come and see the cat, and I said I'd be right over. The man sounded quite desperate, and I hadn't much of importance to do on that lazy Sunday.

I piled my two daughters into the car, and we all went off to meet Mr. Wong and his cat. The girls were eager to see what magic their father could do.

Mr. Wong, a prosperously plump gentleman with a face that looked as though it wanted to be cheerful but was quite unhappy at the moment, led us into the restaurant kitchen. It was the semi-lull between lunchtime and the dinner hour, and his kitchen helpers were cleaning pots and setting up for another frantic round of work.

"There he is," said Mr. Wong, pointing at a large round blob on a shelf near the huge restaurant stove, "and there he's been. Before, he was constipated. He wasn't using his litter pan. I think he was in pain. Now, he doesn't even try to move."

"Mmmhmm," I said. "Been there two days, you say." I looked at the cat, a nondescript Domestic Shorthair about twelve years old, with dust literally gathering on his fur. For a moment, I thought he might be dead already, but when I bent over to pet him gently I could feel his substantial body rising and falling ever so slightly. Other than that, he didn't so much as twitch.

"What does he eat?" I asked.

Mr. Wong's worried face creased into a smile.

"Chinese food," he said.

One of my daughters snickered. I ignored her.

"Perhaps too much of it," I observed.

I knew I was looking at one sick and miserable cat.

My first move was to take the cat's temperature. No sooner had I inserted a thermometer into his rectum than the cat suddenly became galvanized into life as if attacked by a cattle prod. He bounded onto the stove top, leapfrogged over the pots and woks, which fortunately were covered—fortunately, because at this inappropriate time he got a sudden and severe case of diarrhea and started squirting on everything in sight—and slid over a pristine work surface leaving a noxious trail behind him.

"Oh, gross," said Betsy, admiringly. Mr. Wong let out a wail and chased after the cat; the cat darted out of the kitchen and down a basement stairway.

"Wow, that's some magic, Daddy," Leslie said. I thought this was rather sardonic in a young lady of her age.

Mr. Wong came up from the basement, panting.

"He's hiding," he said briefly. "Now I must clean up here before people start coming. You will forgive me, please."

I would have to, and I thought he'd actually been quite lucky. If it had been later in the day, and if those pots had been open and simmering away with Lobster Cantonese and Hot and Sour Soup and Buddha's Delight and Happy Family and General Tso's Chicken . . . I shuddered to think of it. Gross, indeed.

I made a date with Mr. Wong to come to my office with Mao Mao first thing the next morning; that is, if he could find him. Mr. Wong, busily directing his cleanup troops, distractedly agreed. He would find the cat and put him in a box and bring him in. I was a little skeptical. Cats are not easily found when they don't want to be.

To my surprise, when I arrived at my clinic at eight A.M. Monday, the rotund Mr. Wong and his rotund cat were already there.

Mao Mao was an unresisting but heavy bundle when I took him out of his box. This time I managed to take his temperature without incident. It was 104. And he was severely dehydrated. When I palpated his abdomen, I could feel something suspicious in the area of his intestinal tract, a presence of some sort that shouldn't have been there. We X-rayed him to see whether he might perhaps have swallowed a foreign body, possibly string or yarn or maybe a piece of bone.

It was an amorphous image. There was definitely something out of place there, but we couldn't tell what it was.

"Any ideas, Mr. Wong? What could he have swallowed? What does he most like to eat?"

Mr. Wong rumpled his brow. "He likes the skin of roasted duck. With some fat on it. Occasionally we give it to him as a treat. But if you're thinking of string or bone, I am always careful to remove it. Although I must say that everybody likes to spoil him. Sometimes one of the kitchen staff might toss him a little extra without being careful enough."

Whatever it was, we had to get into it. We put Mao Mao on intravenous solution to start him on antibiotics right away, and prepared him for surgery. But first, I had to make my little speech: "Mr. Wong, your cat is seriously overweight. And I have to tell you that excess body fat absorbs anesthesia like a thirsty sponge. Which means that we have to use more of it to put him under—and that, in turn, means that the risk of complications caused by anesthesia is significantly increased. I just wanted you to know."

Mr. Wong thoughtfully stroked his cheeks.

"Is there a choice?"

"No."

"Then let us go ahead."

We removed a knotted piece of butcher's twine, about eighteen inches long, with bits of duck skin still attached, from Mao Mao's small intestine. The area where it had been was infected and inflamed, but when we had cleaned it up, I was confident that the antibiotics would take care of the infection.

Mr. Wong stared silently at the twine when we showed it to him and just shook his head.

"I think maybe there should be a little change in his eating habits from now on," I said. "No more duck skin, no more duck fat and a lot less of the rest of his food. Obesity strains the joints, the ligaments, the heart, the liver, the lungs—virtually every organ of the body. He seems like a nice cat, Mr. Wong, when he isn't messing up the kitchen. Let's keep him alive."

Mr. Wong nodded vigorously.

I also suggested, as diplomatically as I knew how, that the fussy Health Department might prefer to have cats kept out of restaurant kitchens, and he nodded again.

"From now on, upstairs, over the store," he said. "Or in the basement with the mice."

Mice? Whatever. I had done my civic duty.

Mao Mao, for all his heft, made a spectacular recovery after the obstruction was removed and left the hospital five days after surgery with antibiotics to be taken orally. I saw him once again, for a checkup, but never again at the restaurant.

Alice and Ms. Ryan came back for a checkup on schedule and continued to come in weekly for several weeks. Our routine was to give the cat the once-over to make sure that her health was holding up and weigh her to see how much weight, if any, she had lost, so that we could regulate the diet accordingly.

As I had hoped, we were able to put her on the baby scale. The loss was barely perceptible at first, but at least she was no longer gaining. We began to notice that, after we had weighed Alice and were tucking her back into her carrying case, Ms. Ryan stepped daintily onto the platform scale when she thought no one was looking and cautiously weighed herself.

By the second week, I had prescribed an exercise program in which Alice was to run after a Ping-Pong ball for about an hour each day, which meant that somebody had to start the ball rolling for her. She loved it; I don't think she had ever been actively played with before. During that week, she lost her first half pound.

It took about four months for her to drop five pounds, and we were tremendously encouraged. She was beginning to look like a real cat again.

At the end of seven months, she was down to a svelte ten pounds. Ms. Ryan beamed with quiet pride, and the whole office staff cheered with delight.

Now we were able to get Alice going on a maintenance diet. Just as we had eased her onto her weight reduction program, so could we ease her back onto complete and balanced meals—much smaller than she'd been accustomed to. Ms. Ryan would get a baby scale for the cat and do a weight check every two or three weeks.

Of course, what the world wanted to know was: Had Ms. Ryan lost a comparable amount of weight?

We all agreed that she did look slimmer. She really had trimmed down. But how much weight had she actually lost? We never caught a glimpse of the reading on the platform scale, and we never did find out.

But then, it wasn't our business at all. Was it?

CHAPTER ELEVEN

Unwholesome Appetites *and* Addictions

AS A RULE, CATS ARE PRETTY CONSERVATIVE creatures, though a few have been known to stray from the path of virtue. Roberta was such a one. Almost perfect though she was, she had a little failing. She was a rare and magnificent Korat with a silver-blue short coat and large, expressive green eyes; a cheerful breed of cat reputed to bring happiness, prosperity and good luck to the people with whom it lives. The convivial Roberta lived with Matt and Mimi Harrison in a wonderful apartment in the River House on Fifty-second Street, just a block away from my clinic. This cooperative apartment building on the East River has a nice private garden, where residents can walk their pets or sit and appreciate the scenery. Mimi often sat there, cat on her lap, reading and enjoying the surrounding mid-city greenery.

The Harrisons already had, it might be observed, quite a lot of good luck and prosperity. What more could one little cat do?

The Korat cat is a native of Thailand. Matt was in the importing business, and on a trip to Asia the Harrisons bought a kitten in Bangkok. They called her Roberta. Actually, Roberta III. Now, Roberta is not what you might call a traditionally Thai type of name, but Mimi was a sentimentalist. Either that, or she wasn't much good at naming names. Mimi's first cat had been a Roberta; and when she had gone to cat heaven, her successor was called Roberta, as was the next kitty, Roberta from Thailand.

It was the Harrisons' custom to have a Manhattan cocktail or two before dinner, and of course Roberta the good-luck happy cat was an important participant in the Happy Hour.

She was a playful cat, interested in fine foods and very much a member of the family. Mimi would say: "Roberta, would you like some pâté?" At her eager look, Mimi would put a little liver pâté or caviar paste on a cracker, lay it on the sumptuous Oriental carpet and watch fondly as Roberta daintily licked up her treat. Her opinion was asked: "What do you think of the pâté?" Usually the answer was "Purr-yum!" Or at least that's what the Harrisons told me. Their kitty loved the hors d'oeuvres.

Roberta also acquired a fondness for the maraschino cherries in the bottom of the Manhattan glasses. "Want a cherry?" Matt would ask, then fish the cherry out of his drink and roll it on the floor. Roberta would pounce on the cherry and play with it like a little ball. Then she would eat it. The cherries were sweet, and she happened to like some sweet things; and of course those cherries were saturated with alcohol. One or even two cherries wouldn't really harm the cat, but in time she seemed to develop a lust for them . . . or what they were soaked in.

One evening at cocktail time, the doorbell rang—a messenger with a package. As Matt went to another room to find change to tip the man, Mimi took the package to the kitchen. That left the coast clear for Roberta.

Zip! She hopped gracefully onto the coffee table.

The messenger gone, Matt and Mimi came back to the living room. Matt peered into his Waterford cocktail glass.

"I'd have sworn I still had a Manhattan," Matt said, puzzled. "Oh, well."

It was my evening to work late at the clinic. The phone rang. A frantic Mimi cried: "Thank heaven you're there! Something's terribly wrong with Roberta! She's reeling and stumbling, losing her balance and falling down. Could she be having some sort of fit?"

"Bring her right over," I said.

Five minutes later, the Harrisons arrived with Roberta in her carrier. As Matt set it on the examining table and opened it up, I knew it didn't need a Sherlock to tell what ailed Roberta. I lifted a sleepy eyelid, propped open the slack mouth, but even that was unnecessary. The fumes of booze—yes, *booze*—emanating from the carrier announced that Roberta was intoxicated.

I asked a few pointed questions, and the Case of the Missing Manhattan was solved.

"Roberta's just had a little too much to drink," I explained. "Take her home and let her sleep it off."

After promising to monitor Roberta's intake more closely in the future and cut down on the cherries, the chagrined and somewhat embarrassed Harrisons took their cat home. I think they were abashed to learn that their aristocratic Korat was just a common drunk. I had my suspicions that a certain tiddliness, never this bad, had happened before, but I doubted that we had anything to worry about. Cats can develop cirrhosis of the liver, but alcoholism is not common in four-legged creatures.

Perhaps this item from the *Daily News* of January 8, 1993, would be something for the Harrisons and other Twelve-Step-pet owners to consider: near-beer for pets.

"STRASBOURG, FRANCE—A French beer maker, hoping to corner the pet market, has come up with a nonalcoholic, high-energy brew for cats and dogs. The Pecheur brewery's latest creation is made from ingredients left over from the beer-making process and enriched with vitamins and mineral salts. The drink, developed in consultation with veterinarians, will be test marketed in Japan, and if it gets a paws up will be introduced in France and Germany. Pecheur has also experimented with a beer containing malt whiskey and another promoted as an aphrodisiac."

The animal world is still waiting. My human clients often ask me: Don't cats instinctively know what's good for them to eat? I believe that, in the wild, for the most part, they do. As to household pets, I don't think so. Their whole perspective changes when they roam through the department store of indoor life. They eat what they feel like putting in their experimental little mouths. I have said that cats are essentially conservative, but nonetheless many of them scarf down a lot of inappropriate things in addition to real food and sometimes get quite sick. Which is why we often have the problem of removing foreign bodies from cats, such as needles—very high on the list—whole pipe cleaners, peach pits, thimbles, string, rubber bands, paper clips, pieces of house plant, small toys . . . once I even had to remove a plastic knife that had come with a child's dinner party set and mysteriously vanished.

A lot of swallowing emergencies happen during the Christmas season. No wonder. Any number of substances dangerous to cats are in the house at the same time: tinsel on the tree, mistletoe, poinsettias and amaryllis. All can prove perilous if cats ingest them. Once I had Pawline in for a bit of tinsel, and another time for an ornament hook. But those things are fairly routine.

Less routine was the case of Nanook.

Marjorie Miller is a senior sportswear buyer at a major New York department store. She was throwing her annual holiday party in her three-and-a-half-room apartment, filling about twice as much space as she actually had. It was your typical year-end cocktail party: friends from work, old college buddies, newer friends as well, and conspicuous consumption by almost all.

The party, as I was to learn, was a great success—wall to wall people, loud music, louder talking to rise over the music, and lots of nibbling and drinking. Marjorie's Snowshoe cat, Nanook, was then three years old. This is a rare and lovely breed, of average size but distinctive in every other way. The coat is seal point, or fawn-colored, with white markings, often in the form of a dickey; they have white boots on all four feet, and large, bright blue eyes. And the temperament is loving and friendly. Nanook, always one to work a crowd, had been a great hit at the previous year's party, and the guests were eager to see this beautiful and friendly cat again.

But at the height of the merriment, a guest noticed that Nanook was having tremors. A cat owner herself, she knew this behavior was abnormal, and she called her hostess over to take a look at the Snowshoe. He was literally shaking in his boots.

Marjorie thought that Nanook may have snacked on some of the rich food she was serving, but it seemed unlikely. That was not his style. And anyway, if overeating was the problem, the cat would throw up or have a stomachache; he wouldn't have tremors.

She called me at once. I could hear the din of the party in the background, and it sounded very jolly to me. Nanook's condition did not. I told Marjorie to bring Nanook to the clinic right away. She left her party in the hands of a good friend and dashed over immediately.

I've had a number of free-spirited clients, even hippies. After examining Nanook, I had my suspicions. He wasn't drunk, he wasn't overstuffed, he wasn't in pain, he was . . . high? Something else? Whatever else, he was breathing slowly . . . and spaced out. I asked Marjorie if any of the guests had been smoking pot.

"Yes," she admitted. "But Nanook had no way of getting it. Surely, not just the inhaling? . . . "

"I think not," I said. "Just to be on the safe side, let's keep him here overnight. I'll get him to vomit, to see if my conjecture is correct." In my experience with cats on pot—admittedly limited—I have found that the most common symptoms are depression and slow respiration. So it was possible I was wrong about Nanook.

I wasn't. After Marjorie had left, we gave the cat a quarter tea-spoonful of ipecac to cause vomiting. We did this three times, five minutes apart, and about five minutes after the last dose—success! Up came cigarette paper and a lot of odd-looking stuff that could be marijuana. I, of course, couldn't be sure of that without corroborative evidence. We gave Nanook intravenous fluids and a mild sedative to stop the tremors. By the next morning he'd completely recovered.

An anxious Marjorie called me soon after I'd checked him out. Cleaning up after the party, she said, she'd found loose marijuana on the floor. Putting one and one together, she concluded that someone had somehow dropped a joint, and Nanook had found it. And eaten it.

Well, that's a cat for you. He wasn't looking for a gourmet experience or a high, but just something unusual to investigate. And marijuana in any form can't be considered cat-safe. Lecture: When you have cats, you must always be aware of their environment and any dangers posed. Cats are such inquisitive individuals, you just can't put temptation in their way.

That was one holiday experience. Then there was another.

A woman came into the clinic with a very sick cat. He'd been re-fusing food and vomiting for a few days before she brought him in. Joan Watson said that her granddaughter had been visiting at Christ-mas and had played jacks with a set she'd gotten in her stocking. Mrs. Watson thought that perhaps her cat, Horatio, had swallowed a jack, leading to his troubles.

Examining Horatio, I thought she was probably right. But to my surprise, an X ray showed a fishhook in his stomach. Here we had a genuine and painful emergency, and not something from a kiddy stocking. We gave Horatio a tranquilizer to relax him, then passed an endotracheal tube through his mouth into the trachea. This allowed us to give him anesthesia and oxygen directly into the lungs, the same procedure used on people. When the cat was asleep and breathing evenly, we clipped the hair on the abdomen and chest, washed the skin with an antiseptic soap, rinsed it thoroughly and painted the area with antiseptic solution to kill any lingering germs. We then clamped four hand towels, similar to dish towels, to the incision area and then placed over that area a large sterile sheet with an opening through which we would work. This is what we call a drape.

I found the fishhook immediately in Horatio's stomach. But there was more. The kitty had swallowed fishing line as well as the hook, and plenty of it. The line was a sturdy and almost indestructible length of nylon that had migrated into the small intestine, which is approximately three times the length of the body. And here was an extraordinary sight: The line had knotted up a long section of the intestine, resulting in an accordion-like puckering of that organ into a sort of internal cat's cradle. Several very careful incisions were necessary to remove the line without doing further damage to the intestine.

The intestine unpuckered even as we worked.

Horatio had great recuperative powers and was ready to leave the clinic four days after surgery, feeling enormously better. Mrs. Watson, picking him up, told me she'd recalled taking the cat to visit her sister, whose husband's hobby was fishing. Horatio must have wandered into a closet, she thought, been attracted to the fishing line and swallowed it with hook attached. Poor Horatio! Making a meal of hook, line, but thankfully, no sinker.

But it doesn't take a holiday season or a Happy Hour to get even the savviest cat into trouble. I had a client named Jack Reilly, who owned a garage on Ninety-sixth Street about forty-four city blocks from my clinic. Jack took care of my car, and I often gassed up at his place when I drove into the city. I, in turn, took care of Jack's cat, Manny, a black Domestic Shorthair, which we had vaccinated and neutered at the clinic. Manny, in *his* turn, was a working cat who lived in the garage and looked after it.

Jack, a rough diamond of a fellow, was very fond of his cat and treated him royally. He'd call up one of the clinic's secretaries on a regular basis and order up a case or two of the best quality cat food you could buy anywhere, and we'd send it up to Jack's garage by UPS. This perfectly balanced diet was supplemented each Monday with a piece of roast chicken, the remains of the Reillys' Sunday dinner. Nothing was too good for Manny! He was one of the gang at the garage, on call twenty-four hours a day, seven days a week, always ready to pounce into action.

He was a ratter, was Manny; that was his job. In fact, Jack had gotten a cat especially because of a huge rat infestation. But after Manny arrived, no one ever saw a rat or a mouse again.

This tough cat shared something with the dainty Roberta. His downfall was alcohol. But not of the party kind.

One early spring day, Jack happened to see Manny drinking from a pan of antifreeze that had just been drained from a car while the radiator was being repaired. That could not be good for the cat, Jack thought. With the word "poison" ringing in his head, he yanked Manny away from it and called me.

"It's harmful, isn't it?"

"You're absolutely right, it is," I said. "Bring him here immediately. Don't hesitate! *Immediately!* Antifreeze is terribly poisonous. Get him here!"

I told Mickey at Reception to let me know the instant Jack and Manny arrived and went briefly back to my routine. It was a particularly noisy day in New York, I thought. There were sirens out there, and tires were screeching, and Heaven only knew what all was going on.

Mickey burst in and said, "They're here!"

It seemed that I'd no sooner hung up the phone than Jack and

Manny were on the doorstep. I said, "How did you possibly get here so fast? And in noontime traffic?"

"Hey," said Jack, lifting Manny out of his carrier, "I used my New York City influence."

My tech and I got Manny onto a table right away and rounded up the treatments we would be using on him.

"Influence?"

"Yeah, as it happened, when I called you, a police car was in the garage, getting gassed up. I told the guy about the emergency. 'We won't let anything happen to Manny!' is what the cop said. 'Grab him and get in.'"

Thus it was that Jack and Manny were delivered to the clinic with siren wailing, brakes screeching and tires squealing. And people say New York doesn't have a heart!

The prognosis is best, in antifreeze cases, when you get the cat to vomit as soon as possible. We gave Manny syrup of ipecac to induce vomiting, a saline cathartic orally by stomach tube to speed the purging process, and a solution of twenty percent ethanol to dissolve the deadly crystals formed in the kidneys by the antifreeze. Ethanol, I might point out, is drinkable alcohol, and veterinarians have been known to use vodka as an antifreeze antidote.

These procedures were done immediately, virtually simultaneously. Antifreeze is about ninety-five percent ethylene glycol, which is extremely poisonous and rapidly absorbed. What we had to do as quickly as possible was get the poison out, correct the dehydration caused by the antifreeze, and also—because the poison travels to the kidneys—cause urinary excretion.

We kept Manny in the hospital for two days on intravenous fluids. He was not a happy fellow, but his life was charmed. It was very lucky that Jack had noticed the cat slurping up the antifreeze, and just as lucky that the police car was there at the right time. The minimum lethal dose of ethylene glycol mixed fifty percent with water, the way it is when drained from a radiator, is half an ounce. We figured that

Manny had drunk at least that amount. Thanks to quick action on Jack's part and speedy transportation by the NYPD, Manny made an uneventful recovery.

And Jack's garage is still rat-free.

Note: The ethylene glycol antifreeze that Manny lapped up is sweet, which appealed to him. The stuff is also hazardous to dogs and children. Everyone, particularly pet lovers, should know that, when changing antifreeze, all waste should be collected and disposed of safely. Containers of the coolant should never be left unattended. If a car leaks a gray-green fluid on street or driveway, the leakage should be flushed away and the radiator repaired at once.

Auto owners can now buy a safer antifreeze, the less toxic propylene-glycol, sold under the names Sierra and Sta-Clean. To find out where these brands are available, call:

Sierra: Safe Brands Corporation, 1-800-289-7234

Sta-Clean: Sta-Clean Products, 1-800-825-3464.

CHAPTER TWELVE

The Nine Lives
of the Cat, *or*
The Frozen Meow

THAT'S AMAZING," SAID NANCY. "So cats really do have nine lives. Although I think Pawline has used up about fifteen."

"She's done very well," I agreed, as Nancy tucked my favorite cat back into her carrying case. "But the thing about her is, she hardly ever gets into really life-threatening situations."

"I didn't like this one," Nancy said. "When I saw those little bloody flecks coming out of her nose—"

She panicked, and called me.

A very ordinary but nonetheless remarkable thing had happened. Pawline had fallen downstairs, without so much as touching a step. She had been on the second-floor landing of the Gardner house about to take a leap onto the middle of the spiral staircase and then, as was her custom, take another leap onto the parlor floor. But this time, as she poised herself on the edge of the stairwell, she was disturbed by a horrendous crashing sound—I never did find out what it was—which startled her into losing her concentration altogether and sent her crashing down onto the floor.

Cats are pretty good at calculating distances, and Pawline was right up there with the best of them, but she did tend to be sensitive to sudden moves and unexpected loud noises. Nancy saw her plummeting to the floor, unprepared for impact; landing badly, staggering to her feet, shaking her head as if dazed. Nancy ran toward her, noticing to her horror that a few little flecks of what looked like watery blood were flying out of her nose.

So here we were again. Nancy thought Pawline was bleeding from her brain, but Nancy always did tend to have a colorful view of events. I saw no trace of blood when I examined the cat and concluded that she must have had a tiny nosebleed. Nor was there any damage to her head, her legs or the rest of her body.

"She's just had a shock," I said. "But she's fine. Keep an eye on her for a day or two to make sure her behavior is normal. If you notice anything, call me."

The fact of the matter is that, even though Pawline had been given her name as a pun on *The Perils of Pauline* because she tended to get herself involved in perilous situations, she was not quite the most trouble-prone cat I had ever known. Most of her disasters were small ones. The episode with Mrs. McGonigle had been really serious, but that wasn't Pawline's fault. Getting stuck in the neighbor's drainpipe wasn't good . . . the paw in the mousetrap was really quite dumb . . . the incident of the gas oven was—well, that could have been a nasty one. It was an old stove, and one day John Gardner had turned on the gas, opened the oven door, stuck a lighted match inside and seen in the back of the oven—two gleaming eyes! Next thing he knew, he had a cat streaking over his shoulder.

But if I were to look at a nine-lifer, Mollie Jones would be at the head of my list. Sweet, demure and dangerous Mollie.

Mollie is a trim little red Abyssinian, only four months old when she began her career as an adventuress. Her owner was Priscilla Jones, a very conscientious cat lover who adored her.

Our first meeting was a standard, uneventful checkup. The next had to do with an incident in the Jones family kitchen.

One morning, Priscilla Jones took some food out of the freezer and put it on the counter top along with several other items that she was planning to transform into lunch for a guest. The freezer was in the lower part of the refrigerator directly opposite from where she was working and perhaps two feet away. As was her custom, Mrs. Jones kicked the freezer door shut behind her with a neat little motion of her foot, not looking back as she did so. It closed with the usual satisfying thunk.

Working quickly, as she always did, Mrs. Jones assembled her materials and covered them to await her return from the local bakery. At the Well-Bread Loaf, she ran into a friend and chatted a while; came back, checked the mail, took the still-warm bread into the kitchen and answered the ringing telephone. As she talked, she became aware of a loud and insistent meow coming from . . . she couldn't figure out where. Walking around with the long telephone cord variously stretching and trailing, she looked under tables and behind doors and finally gave up on trying to do two things at once.

"Goodbye, Mother," she said, and then she really started looking. Mollie was trapped some place. Meowrrr! Mollie was quite upset. But where was she? A loud and panicky but oddly muffled howl came from the—the refrigerator? the freezer? The freezer!

Mrs. Jones opened the door and a pathetic, shivering but indignant little creature hopped out, whiskers stiff and back hair standing on end. "Oh, you are a very cold kitty," said Mrs. Jones, and she was indeed. She could have been a very frozen kitty if Mrs. Jones hadn't found her in time.

Mollie gave her a look, the way that cats do.

"Hey, it's not my fault," said Mrs. Jones.

She wrapped the cat in a warm towel and called me.

"You've done the right thing," I told her. "But bring her in later, if you want to."

The conscientious Mrs. Jones did bring her in. The cat was all thawed out and she was not developing galloping pneumonia, and we—Mrs. Jones and I—shared little stories about curiosity killing the cat, and that was that for then.

About two weeks later, Mollie was in our waiting room sitting in Mrs. Jones's lap waiting for her vaccinations. It's a large room, with twelve individual chairs and a couple of benches, but the clients were more than usually bunched together to avoid the far left-hand corner of the room where the radiator was situated. We had blocked off this area with large pieces of plywood because there was a leak in the radiator, and the floor beneath and around it had to be fixed. Naturally, I didn't want any people or animals straying into the scene before the job was done.

But! . . . Inquisitive little Mollie jumped out of her owner's arms, over the plywood barrier and down into the hole next to the pipe for the radiator, which went into the space between the floor and the basement ceiling. The opening was just large enough to get your arm into—or your cat, as the case may be—but too small and dark to look through.

Thumps! Shrieks!

I came racing out of Examination Room Three to see what the commotion was all about.

Mrs. Jones was having a fit. "Get my cat!" she kept screaming. "Get my cat out of there!" Bruno, Ms. Gargiulo's Great Dane, was booming with alarm, and somebody's little terrier was yapping. "Oh, my goodness," said old Mrs. Bailey, "oh, my goodness!" "My cat, my cat, get my cat out of there!" screeched Mrs. Jones, pointing at the radiator hole.

My heart sank. I had visions of tearing up the whole floor to get darling Mollie out.

"We'll get her, Mrs. Jones," I said soothingly. "But she's not going to come out while all this disturbance is going on. Why don't you just go on home? Leave her here. As soon as things settle down, we'll try to get her out. Look at it this way: If she has to be trapped anyplace, it might as well be in her doctor's office, right?"

She didn't crack a smile. Neither did I. Tearing up the waiting room floor would be quite a job. It could take weeks to get it pulled out and replaced. I was still waiting for the plumber . . . Oh, the plumber. Maybe he'd have an idea.

After Mrs. Jones had left, more or less calmed down, we called the plumber. Several times. He was unavailable for comment.

As soon as all our appointments were done and all clients had left, we got back to the problem of Mollie. Three of us, cat specialists all, took turns making enticing sounds down the hole. Mollie was not enticed. Once in a while we heard a very faint chirrup coming from a far corner of the floor, but all that meant was that she was still alive. I knew she was; I knew she was all right. Nervous, probably feeling a tad embarrassed in a feline sort of way—they don't like to be caught in the act of doing something foolish—and probably getting a little hungry. But otherwise fine.

We decided to put some food down the hole and a bit more up on the edge, on the theory that she would nibble it at the bottom and then come up for more. Or if she could be seen taking the food down below, someone with a long, thin arm could reach in, take hold of her and haul her up.

When my night tech, Jose, came in, I explained what had been happening, and he said he'd wait up all night for her. I surveyed him critically. He had suitably thin arms, slender but sinewy.

Next morning: I was in very early. Jose was weary. No Mollie had appeared. The food at the edge of the hole was untouched. Jose said that during the night, he had heard Mollie walking around under the floor, but she hadn't come to the opening.

"Well, let's try this," I said. I took a cat food can out of the supermarket bag I'd brought with me. "Maybe something a little more exotic in the food line. She must be getting hungry by now."

I popped the lid of a particularly odorous canned mackerel and scooped some of the smelly stuff down into the hole.

"Let's back off now. I won't put any up on the edge; we'll just wait and see what happens. And if she shows up—pounce!"

We sat unmoving and in absolute silence for maybe minutes, maybe half an hour. After a while we heard little scrabbling sounds below; and then some sucking, lip-smacking noises.

She was ravenous for the stuff.

"Now," I whispered softly. "If you see her . . . "

Jose slid forward, very quietly; peered down the hole. His eyes lit up and his eyebrows rose. "I see her eating . . . now I see her tail . . . now I—"

Grab her by the hind leg!

She came up yowling and scratched him.

I pulled the cat away from him, said, "You wash that down with antiseptic right away!" and popped the cat into a cage. She was absolutely fine but for a little fit of pique.

Mrs. Jones, when I called her, was thrilled with our success and apologetic for having become hysterical. All was to be forgiven and forgotten.

I really did like Mollie. I wasn't looking forward to seeing her any time soon, but I thought her a very upbeat cat—outgoing, affectionate and inquisitive, to say the least.

When I next saw Mollie, the Joneses were living on the ninth floor of a pleasant old apartment building, complete with terraces for all and a doorman who chanced to be another client of mine. The Joneses had chosen the building because they thought the terrace would be a great place for Mollie to go out and get some supervised exercise.

There were two French doors leading from the living room to the terrace, and it made for a very attractive scene. But, knowing Mollie's penchant for running into trouble, the Joneses kept the doors open only when they were in the house and could observe her on the terrace.

One summer's day, when Priscilla and her husband, Jay, left the apartment together, they somehow failed to close the terrace doors as firmly as they usually did. Reconstructing the scene later, they figured that Mollie had been able to push a door open with her nose and squeeze out onto the terrace when no one was around to stop her. Then, probably, she got up onto the metal railing that topped the brick wall surrounding the terrace and perched there or, more likely, strolled around on it to view the sights of the neighborhood.

Then something happened. She may have been frightened by a bird or a loud noise or the screech of a car on the street or some other city activity. Whatever it was, she lost her footing and fell. Luckily, the terrace on the seventh floor had a large awning. Mollie landed on it like an acrobat hitting a trampoline, slightly breaking her fall, then bounced up over the edge and plunged down the remaining flights to land in the garden shrubbery. Her really lucky break was the appearance of a woman passerby who saw the last part of her fall, hard landing and all, and ran inside the building to report it.

Simon the doorman knew at once whose cat it was. He also knew that the Joneses were not at home. Thanking the woman for caring enough to help—she said she had cats of her own—he went outside to take a quick look for himself and then called my clinic.

It sounded pretty bad to me. She could be in shock, she was certainly frightened, and she might possibly have fractures.

"Could you get her over here somehow?"

He said he could. "I'll take my lunch break now," he said.

I told him to wrap a towel around Mollie very carefully, lift her up gently and bring her straight to the clinic.

It had been a sudden, awkward landing from the ninth floor, and I expected the worst—fractured bones, perhaps, internal hemorrhages, severely injured paws—but when I examined Mollie I was surprised and relieved to see that the damage was minimal. She was in shock, the nails of all four paws were broken and bleeding, and her nose was bleeding, too. But there were no internal hemorrhages, no fractures, not even a broken tooth.

A miracle, I thought.

We put Mollie on intravenous fluids to treat her for shock, stopped the bleeding and kept her in the hospital overnight.

I was certain she'd be able to leave in the morning.

Mrs. Jones didn't wait until morning. When Simon told her what had happened, she came right to our hospital and stayed there until midnight with Mollie and Erin, the tech on night duty. Dr. Barton, my associate who lived in the building, checked Mollie several times during the night until he was positive she was out of danger. Mrs. Jones left, to return in the morning; Erin stayed with Mollie.

And Mollie was fine. Famished, a little testy about what we had put her through and ready to go home. Mrs. Jones and I figured that she'd used up three of her nine lives, and Mrs. Jones was determined that she'd not use up any more.

Whether she did or not—that's another story.

Mollie's plunge was a typical case of high-rise syndrome, which is characteristic of summer in New York. People living in high places tend to leave their windows open in the summertime to catch the breezes, unworried that burglars might scale the heights, and even screenless because high-flying insects are few. Animals, particularly cats, tend to take advantage of this open invitation to the outdoors. Sometimes the phenomenon reaches epidemic proportions. Literally hundreds of animals, from cats and dogs to the occasional iguana and turtle, skydive without parachutes and wind up on city sidewalks suffering from "extreme vertical deceleration trauma"—namely, crash landing. But cats, with their flexible spines and finely honed righting reflexes, are excellent survivors.

What I found so fascinating about Mollie's fall was that it was just the wrong distance for a safe landing, and yet she had come out of it relatively unscathed. But that's a survivor for you.

Several years ago, a group of veterinarians attached to New York City's Animal Medical Center published a research paper on the highrise syndrome, reported in *The New York Times*, in which they concluded that cats falling from five to nine stories suffer the worst damage—broken bones, head trauma, internal injuries—whereas cats falling thirty stories or more somehow escape with nothing worse than a nosebleed when their head hits the ground after the rest of the body lands.

How could this be possible?

The same study observes that a cat who falls from a building achieves a terminal velocity of sixty miles per hour—half that of humans—at about five stories down, so the impact is never greater than what would be induced by that speed. Having reached terminal velocity, a startled cat falling from the ninth floor starts to right itself and braces for landing, hitting the ground legs forward, breaking them and injuring its chest and lungs in the process. The impact at such close range can be horrendous.

But with more room to spare, a cat falling from thirty stories or even higher has time to prepare and relaxes, at which time it spreads its limbs wide like a flying squirrel, flattening and cushioning its body for landing, thus diminishing the shock to any one of its parts.

One summer month in New York—July 1994—Leo the cat, not one of my patients, strolled onto the forty-sixth floor terrace of his Manhattan apartment while his owner was walking the dog outside, peered over the edge, and—zoom! Splat!

Leo landed in a planter and survived. Forty-six floors! Winded, but not much worse than that. I figure that trip took up at least half of his lives.

To me, this ability to adapt and survive is truly one of nature's miracles. Thinking of Mollie and Leo, I am reminded of the number of cats I have known, many of them strays, who have had limbs broken and reset by happenstance, and others who have had legs amputated either by accident or because of mutilation or cancer.

Is their psyche damaged? I really don't think so.

One such physically damaged cat is Dodger. Dodger is a cheerful black-and-white streak who races up circular staircases, frolics on the rocky outcropping alongside his house and engages in spirited scuffles with the two other cats in his household. All this is normal cat behavior; so normal that when I first visited his home as a guest, I didn't realize at once that Dodger is a three-legged cat. His right front leg was amputated after a diagnosis of bone cancer. If his self-esteem has been crushed, it doesn't show. He doesn't know he's been short-changed; nothing else in his life is lacking.

I have met many Dodgers, Tripods, Long Johns and Peg Legs in my time, all of them loved and loving, and I am always struck by how much they enjoy life. Cats can triumph over even major traumas; cats are infinitely resilient, so long as they are loved.

The fact is, some of these nine-lifer cats have more of a life than some of the people I know.

CHAPTER THIRTEEN

Can You Catch It *from* Your Cat?

V
IVIAN ROGERS WAS A GLAMOROUS, beautiful client who owned an almost equally stunning White Persian cat, which she herself combed and groomed every day. As a result of this loving care, Alma—the cat—at all times looked like the epitome of a show cat ready for her close-up. Ms. Rogers was, and is, something of a show cat herself, an actress who at that time was playing the lead in a Broadway hit. She told me that she probably wouldn't be able to see it through to the end of the run, or at least she would have to take some time off. Her medical doctor had told her that she was pregnant.

"Well, that's wonderful news!" I said. She looked radiant. Then her face dimmed a little.

"That's why we're here," she said. "My physician advised me to have a test for toxoplasmosis, which I did, and said that my cat should be tested, too. He said something about zoonoses, and then went on to talk about my weight and diet and all those other pregnancy things. But I don't understand what's supposed to be the problem with toxoplasmosis, and I don't know what zoonoses is, or are. Is this something I can catch from Alma?"

"Maybe," I said. "If she has it. We'll test her." Alma, on my examination table, was looking in prime condition as always.

"In fact," I added, "we might as well give her a complete checkup while she's here. Now. About your other questions: Zoonoses, plural, are diseases that can be passed from animals to people. Toxoplasmosis is one of them. This is a parasitic disease that can be transmitted in other ways as well, such as by the person handling infected raw meat or ingesting meat that's not fully cooked. In the case of cats, a person can contract it by handling cat feces when cleaning out the kitty-litter box."

"*Handling* them?" said Ms. Rogers, curling her gorgeous upper lip.

"Accidentally," I said. "It happens. Why don't I go ahead and get a blood sample from Alma—"

"Just one minute," Ms. Rogers said, in the authoritative tone she uses when about to contradict her director. (I saw her at rehearsal once. She can be formidable.) "I want to know about that little toxo-parasite. What does it do?"

"Well!" I said. Going instantly into my tutorial mode, I began the lecture I had given to Nancy Gardner, and indeed to all cat-owning women of child-bearing age. "The organism is a minute parasite called *Toxoplasma gondii,* and the disease it carries is toxoplasmosis. In cats, it affects the digestive system and causes diarrhea. In healthy humans with a normally functioning immune system, it has very little effect. But developing fetuses are at risk during the first two trimesters. The parasite can travel through the placenta to the fetus and invade the tissues, and the result may be infection or an abnormality of the fetus or even spontaneous abortion."

"That sounds absolutely terrible. Quite frightening." Ms. Rogers was wringing her eloquent hands, which I have seldom seen people actually do. "I'm sorry I asked."

"You should also know that most cats don't have it, and the transference only occurs if the cat is positive for the disease. Your best protection is good sanitation. If you must clean the kitty-litter box yourself, do it every day and as soon as possible after the cat defecates, because it's only when the oocysts—the toxoplasma eggs—sit around in the environment for more than a day or two that they incubate and become infective. And you should use disposable gloves while gardening or cleaning the litter pan."

Ms. Rogers wrinkled her nose.

"I don't garden in the city, darling, and I'm not really into cleaning out freshly used kitty potties. I suppose it's all right if somebody else does it?"

"It's all right with me. In fact, it's preferable. But make sure it gets done. And by a nonpregnant person who washes his hands afterward."

Ms. Rogers nodded and was silent for a moment, looking thoughtful.

"You'd think," she said eventually, "that my own doctor, my obstetrician, could have explained all this to me. But the fact that he didn't makes me wonder—are there any other diseases I should worry about catching from my cat?"

"Not really," I said, "not so far as your pregnancy goes. But there are some other diseases people can get from cats. Ringworm, for example."

"Worms!"

"Not exactly. Fungi, actually. We'll get to the worms later."

Ms. Rogers rolled her limpid turquoise eyes.

I continued, "Ringworm is a skin fungus infection that a human can get from a cat or *give* to a cat. In humans, it shows up in the form of skin lesions and looks like a little discolored scaly rash, ring-shaped or at least round. Quite small. Sometimes there are several of them in a cluster and they generally itch, though not always."

"Is that right?" Ms. Rogers said thoughtfully. "So she could have a fungus. Well, well. And what else?"

Alma rolled over and tried to sneak off the table.

"Oh, a couple of little things," I said casually. "Roundworms, mange, rabies, plague." The divine Rogers eyebrows shot upward in alarm. "But why don't I just go ahead and take the blood sample before we lose her attention. And the temperature, to get her started."

"Plague?" said Ms. Rogers.

"Bubonic," I said cheerfully. "The black plague. Carried by rodent fleas. But it's very rare, especially among indoor cats. Your doctor would have told you if you had it."

"I am not so sure," Lady Macbeth said ominously.

Alma's temperature was normal, and she gave her little portion of blood as graciously as if she were donating it. She seemed to be as healthy a cat as I was likely to encounter. But there was one little thing that I hadn't observed on her before.

As part of our examination of all cats, we go over them with a black light—which is really an ultraviolet light—to see if there is any sign of ringworm. This is quite a common condition in cats, especially in kittens, and although Alma was no longer a baby, I was particularly interested in what might turn up in view of my discussion with Ms. Rogers.

Tech-of-the-day Julio and I scanned the beautifully groomed furry body with the black light.

"What are you doing?" the imperious voice inquired.

"Looking for ringworm," I answered absently. "If there's a positive area, the black light will show it up . . . There, now, here's something." The left ear was fluorescing in the dark.

"Amazing! What does that mean?"

"It means we're getting a positive indication of ringworm. Has Alma been around any other cats in the past few months?"

Ms. Rogers shook her head. "No, she never gets to meet any other cats. She doesn't go outdoors, and cats don't come to visit us. Somebody could have brought it in, perhaps."

"Maybe. Probably. If you'll just wait here for a second, I'll go into the lab for a tube to do a fungus culture on that lesion in her ear. Be right back."

As it happened, the lab phone rang with some blood results on a seriously ill Maine Coon, and I was slightly delayed in getting back to the examination room.

When I did, I stopped abruptly in the doorway and stood there stock still, absolutely dumbfounded. I don't know where Julio had gone, and I didn't even notice Alma. All I could see was the bare backside of Vivian Rogers.

Ms. Rogers had dropped her pants. She was leaning over the examination table, buck naked from the waist down. The woman was mooning me!

She half-turned her head. "Oh, there you are, Dr. Padwee. I was waiting for you."

"You—you were?"

"Yes, Doctor. Look, I have two spots on my ass. Come on, look. Look closer." She pointed to an area on her backside.

Now I like to think I am reasonably sophisticated, but first of all, people don't usually use the word "ass" in my office when referring to their own posterior, and secondly, they don't usually urge me to look at it.

I moved toward her, cautiously.

"See these spots?" she demanded. "Do you think these could be ringworm?"

At this point, I really did take a close look. Yes, there were lesions. They looked very much like ringworm candidates to me. In fact, they looked exactly like the textbook pictures of the ringworm lesion.

"Ms. Rogers, I do think they could be," I said gratefully—gratefully, because here was a medical condition that I could cope with by foisting it off on someone else. "Nice diagnosis. But you'll have to go to your own medical doctor for diagnosis and treatment. Tell him that we know your cat has got it. And now, if you don't mind—"

She rearranged her clothes like the quick-change artist that she was.

And she said, "How could we both have gotten this disease? How could I have gotten it?"

I shook my head. "I really don't know. It's highly contagious. You could have picked it up visiting someone, on the subway, wherever."

"Subway!" She gave me the haughty look of someone who never uses public transportation. But then she laughed like a teenager. I happen to know, and she knows that I know, that she often uses buses and subways. Limos are for openings, cabs are for lunch dates and shopping, buses and subways are for coming to the vet.

"Well, think about it," I said. "I'll call you tomorrow when we have the toxoplasmosis results."

I called her the next day. "Alma's clean," I said. "No toxoplasmosis. Only the ringworm. Do you have any idea—?"

"Doctor, doctor!" she trilled, interrupting me as usual. "I'm so relieved about the toxo thing. Now, about the ringworm. I think we've got it, by George, I think we've got it!"

"I know we've got it," I said a trifle irritably. "The question is, *where* did we get it?"

I thought I heard a little sigh, and then she told me that not so long ago, she had visited a friend who had acquired a couple of darling little kittens from a pet shop about two months before.

"As it happens, I stayed over that night. There was a blizzard or something, I forget what. And those two sweet little kittens climbed into bed with me. And do you know what I think?"

"I think you think the kittens gave it to you and you gave it to Alma. And what I think is, you're probably right, so if your friend would like to bring in those kittens, we'll give them the test, too. Kittens are really vulnerable to this problem."

"And what about me?" she said kittenishly.

"Oh, well," I said feebly. "Just get everybody checked out, that's all I ask."

I had a new client a couple of days later. She brought the kittens in, and they checked out positive for ringworm. All the cats and all the owners were put on medication, and in a very short time the whole lot were completely cured. Another medical mystery solved!

Ms. Rogers brought Alma in for a checkup a few weeks later and, inquiring after the lady's well-being, I seized this opportunity to elaborate on zoonoses.

"Plague?" I said. "Not to worry. There may be a couple of dozen cases throughout the United States in any given year, usually in rat- or rodent-infested areas. Alma's not going to get it. Neither are you. Roundworms? You can get these only if you're very careless, which we both know you are not. I can check your cat for worms, which I always do, and if necessary I'll worm her. Meanwhile, if you have anything to do with the cat pan—which you're not supposed to!—*wash your hands!*"

Ms. Rogers struck an exaggeratedly defensive pose.

"Rabies. This is the most serious of the zoonotic diseases, and it's always been the most feared because it's a nasty, virulent thing, and the treatment used to be so drastic. It's common in the wildlife population of the United States, among bats, skunks, foxes, raccoons and the like. But you're not going to get it unless your cat happens to get bitten by an infected wild creature and then nips you with a puncture wound, and she's not going to do that because she's vaccinated against rabies. So don't forget the booster shots. And, incidentally, if you do happen to get rabies from some other animal, the treatment is much more tolerable than it used to be."

"Such a relief," Ms. Rogers remarked. "Anything else?"

"Yes, I think you'll like this one. Sarcoptic mange. It has something in common with ringworm. It's caused by a minute little mite that burrows into the skin and creates a whole host of skin conditions, ranging from inflammation to hair loss. And what's cute about it is that, like ringworm, you can give it to your cat and your cat can give it to you."

"I hope that's all," Ms. Rogers said.

"Nearly all. I just want to warn you about one little mite that you may want to look out for. I don't know of any cases of transference, but who knows? Mites, like fleas, are ubiquitous little things. This particular mite is not always easily spotted, unless you happen to be watching closely. It's called a fur mite, and it's also known as walking dandruff because that's what it looks like. En masse, and they always are en masse, these tiny little critters appear to be dry dandruffy scales on a cat's back—ambulatory scales, moving back and forth, forth and back, as if the whole coat were a shifting mass."

"Is *that* all?"

"Oh, almost forgot. There's cat scratch fever. It's exactly what the name implies, except that bites can have the same effect as scratches. You don't always know where those little teeth and claws have been. There aren't any symptoms in the cat, but the cat can transmit bacterial infection to humans. Children are more susceptible than adults. The result can be fever and swelling of the glands. If you should happen to get scratched—"

"Wash it out and call you," Ms. Rogers said with a sigh. I could see I was losing my audience.

"Wash it out and call your own doctor," I said crisply.

"*Now* is there anything else?" she inquired with a touch of hauteur. "Is that really, really all?"

"Other than that," I observed, "there's not much that a human can get from a cat, except a lot of attitude. But you know about that."

There many be another side to the coin, and not just the attitude part. The question arises, Can your cat get it from you?

After the divine Ms. Rogers left, I recalled my visit from George Hoffman. He had brought his gentlemanly Birman, Oscar, into the clinic the week before.

"What's the problem?" I asked. "It's not time for Oscar's usual shots, and he looks in fine shape."

Mr. Hoffman cleared his throat. "This is not something I would ordinarily discuss with you, Dr. Padwee," he said diffidently, "but I have reason to be worried. At least, I think I do. You see, I am gay and I'm worried about AIDS. I've been hearing that cats can get something called Feline AIDS. Can we test Oscar for it? And if he has it, can he transmit it to me?"

This was not the first time that a client had asked me such a question. I hastened to reassure him.

"The 'Cat AIDS' you've heard of is a scary condition called feline immunodeficiency virus, known as FIV. The FIV and HIV viruses cause similar clinical disorders, but that's where the similarity ends. I want to make it crystal clear to you that cats cannot, repeat *cannot*, transmit AIDS. And they can't transmit to humans the feline leukemia virus, which also looks a little like AIDS but isn't. There is a preventive vaccine for the leukemia virus in cats—as you know, because we give it to Oscar and all cats regularly—but there is no preventive vaccine for FIV. If Oscar were to have FIV, or get it, there are effective clinical treatments that may keep him alive and disease-free for several years. But it's quite obvious that Oscar is in the pink, so to speak. And as an indoor cat, having no contact with infected cats, he's extremely unlikely to get FIV. So you need have no worries on that account."

Mr. Hoffman had listened attentively, and his relief was plain. But again the throat clearing, and a little pucker between his brows, showed that he wasn't finished with his questions.

"Um. Of course I'm thrilled with the news about Oscar. But could it be the other way around? Could my cat get AIDS? I ask because my companion has just been diagnosed as HIV positive. Oscar sits on his lap all the time, and even licks his face."

"Again, no," I said. "Oscar's being a good friend. Let him. Cats cannot get AIDS from a human any more than humans can get it from cats. You've got problems in your life, but Oscar is not one of them. Both of you can keep on enjoying his friendship."

I was pleased for them both as they left, but also saddened.

Cats don't know how to worry, but we humans do.

CHAPTER FOURTEEN

Toothsome
Remedies

THIS IS A STORY ABOUT A COUPLE of neighbors with a couple of horses and a cat named Artichoke. One spring evening, my good friend Jeff Minor, who lives about two country miles down the road from my house (that's in the neighborhood, by our reckoning) called me at home to tell me about inheriting his mother's cat. It was a gray male Domestic Shorthair, Jeff said, about four years old, which his mother had called Artichoke because of its large green eyes. Well, I've heard funnier names and less reasonable reasons for them.

Jeff told me he didn't know much about cats or what they were supposed to be like at four years old, and could I examine Artichoke some time? Possibly that evening?

I couldn't do it then because Jane and I had been invited out to dinner, and we were practically out the door when the phone rang, so I offered my apologies and asked him to call again soon. He said he would.

A few days passed without further word from Jeff. Then, on the next Saturday afternoon, when I was busy being Squire Padwee and cultivating my garden, Jeff and his wife, Mary, rode up on their horses. This was not an unusual kind of visit from a neighbor; most of the people in the area had horses and tended to canter around on the country roads with them on weekends.

We greeted the Minors warmly, and then I said, "You should have brought Artichoke with you. This would have been a fine time to check him out."

"As a matter of fact," said Jeff, "we did."

He reached into his saddlebag and brought out a cat that looked as though he didn't much mind how he was being carried around. I gathered from Jeff that Artichoke rather enjoyed a little horsebacking on occasion.

"Actually, we call him Artie," said Jeff.

"How do you do," I said formally. But as soon as that cat was let out of the bag, I sensed this was going to be no ordinary confrontation.

Artie had the quintessential cat face of a tabby but the smoky gray coat of a Russian Blue, which he wasn't. Altogether he was quite a striking-looking cat, but not very large for his four years. Rather small and thin, in fact, I thought. What was he, maybe five and a half, six pounds? Jeff handed him to me.

Yes, he was probably less than six pounds.

And it seemed to me that something else had come out of that saddlebag along with Artie.

"Is there some kind of problem with him?" I asked.

Jeff gave a little bark of laughter and said, "You tell me!"

Artie opened his mouth in a meow, and I nearly fell over. One inadvertent sniff of that cat's breath and I came close to passing out, just like the old anesthetist who had been helping my brother deliver kittens. The odor! Unbelievable! It smelled like something terribly decayed, which something probably was. I looked into the cat's mouth, and I really did recoil. Phew! This breath could strip paint. Decades of veterinary practice, and a cat's breath almost does me in.

"This cat has major halitosis," I said mildly. With my nose so close to his mouth, I truly felt as if I were being gassed. Mary, several feet away, had a pained look on her face.

"We thought it was pretty bad," said Jeff, "but I don't know much about cats. Maybe they all smell like that."

"Believe me, I wouldn't be in practice if they did."

I turned off my nose buds and took a long, slow look inside the pitiful little mouth. The gums were horrifyingly red and inflamed, clearly badly infected, and the teeth were covered with a heavy encrustation of plaque that had hardened into tartar. Here was classic gingivitis, an early stage of periodontal disease . . . or maybe not so early. I could see a couple of loose teeth, possibly abscessed by infection.

"Wow!" I said eloquently. "Have you never brushed his teeth?"

Jeff looked startled. "Are you kidding? Brush a cat's teeth? I don't even brush my horse's teeth."

I ignored that. I don't do horses anymore.

Artichoke could not have been eating a balanced diet for some time. He was too thin, and his gums were too sore.

I inquired about his diet.

Mary said, "Artie's been a very poor eater ever since we got him. I've been feeding him the same thing as Jeff's mother used to feed him—baby food, mostly chicken or beef—but very often he hardly touches it. It's not bad for him, is it?"

"It's quite good in itself, on a short-term basis," I said, "but it doesn't give him everything he needs. Soft food alone tends to bring on dental problems. A cat needs something to sink his teeth into. Look at his gums—they are truly rotting, and his teeth are in bad shape. Just as a matter of interest—has he ever had any dental care?"

Mary took a look, and pulled back involuntarily.

"I don't believe so," she said. "I didn't know cats were supposed to go to the dentist."

"No, but they should have regular checkups with their veterinarian," I said, "and he or she should tell you when the cat's teeth or gums need work."

I looked over Artie's squirming little body for any other visible signs of an ailment, but found none.

"It's possible," I suggested, "that this is an indication of some internal problem, but I don't think so, based on his diet. And at this point, it's not surprising that he's eating very little. With his mouth so inflamed and his gums so infected, he probably finds it too painful to eat anything, even baby food. Dry chow would have been good, but obviously he can't gum that."

I stroked the cat's head, and he let out a blast of effluvium.

"So is this a major problem?" Jeff wanted to know.

"Not necessarily. Gingivitis can be extremely uncomfortable—both for the cat and for the people who want to cuddle it—but if that's all it is, we can take care of it. There's nothing I can do at home, though."

I keep a few emergency supplies in my house, but with very rare exceptions, I don't treat clients at home for anything much more than minor injuries. Certainly I don't have the dental instruments or the anesthetic I would probably need to work on the teeth. Artichoke would have to make a trip to the city.

"Bring him to my hospital first thing Monday morning," I said, tucking Artie back into his saddlebag. "Don't give him anything to eat after midnight Sunday, because what we're going to do to the mouth amounts to an operation. But what you could do now—"

They looked expectant. Artie was making muffled meows in the background.

"—is start him on an antibiotic for the mouth infection. I'll call the village drugstore and phone in a prescription for amoxicillin. This is an antibiotic that comes in pediatric form. It's suitable for cats as well as kids; we often use it."

As a general rule, it is a bad idea to give human medicines to cats. Aspirin—never. Antihistamines—only a few, and only when prescribed. No anti-parasite preparations, unless labeled safe for cats. No antiseptics containing phenol or creosote. No acetaminophen, like Tylenol, Dristan or Nyquil. No ibuprofen, like Advil or Motrin. And no chocolate. But most human antibiotics are safe for cats when prescribed for them. Leftovers from the family medicine cabinet won't do. *Nothing* from the family medicine cabinet will do, except an occasional Q-Tip.

Jeff and Artie arrived at our hospital early Monday morning. I thought it would be a good idea, I told Jeff, if I were to give the cat a complete examination before we did the dental work. I wanted to determine two things: Did this cat have a medical problem that we were overlooking? Was he strong enough to hold up under a general anesthetic?

Artie bore up very well during the preliminaries. Jeff watched us drawing blood and putting the kitty on intravenous fluids, remarked that he was glad I wasn't *his* dentist, and left for work. By that afternoon, we would have the blood test results, and if there were no complications, we would do the dental work in the afternoon. Artichoke would be able to go home on Tuesday morning.

The blood tests came back within the normal range. There were no indications of any internal problems—other than those inside the mouth—and now we could get on with the dentistry. I was most anxious to do it, because this cat had the absolutely worst case of dragon breath I'd ever encountered.

He went under with a soft little snore and breathed easily throughout the procedure. The primary reason for the anesthetic, of course, was to make sure that Artie would feel no pain in his tender gums while we worked, but I might add that, without putting him under, it would have been impossible to do any serious work in his mouth for more than a few seconds. That is not the sort of activity that cats put up with, least of all when their mouths are in as bad condition as Artie's. The scaling process is quite vigorous, and it extends, literally, right under the gums—especially when those gums have been neglected for years and have started to recede.

(An incidental observation: This receding of the gums is also common in the elderly, and it happens to humans as well as other animals. Thus the expression "long in the tooth," to connote an individual somewhat beyond the prime of life.)

Once in a while, clients will tell me that they're able to brush their cat's teeth with little fingertip toothbrushes specially made for the job, or actually pick off plaque with their own fingernails, but I must say few cats allow this sort of thing unless the owner is very patient and gradually gets the cat into the habit of a daily toothbrushing or a regular plaque-picking. It only takes six to eight hours for plaque to form, so the task of removing it at home is endless and thankless.

Using pediatric dental forceps, I split the heavy tartar on Artie's teeth and chipped off the worst of it. The tartar had been accumulating for so long that it was actually pressing against the gums, causing redness and ulceration at the gum line. After we had removed the initial layer, I could actually see the teeth, which I continued to clean with an ultrasound scaler and a fine rinse of spraying water. Then, with a little instrument called a handscaler, I went under the margins of the soft, receding gums and scaled the base of the teeth. Some of them wobbled a little as I worked.

We're in the nick of time, I thought. I hoped.

Finally, or almost finally, I polished the teeth. Now, at last, I could see them clearly . . . all thirty of them, clean and polished and shiny, and ready for close examination.

The looseness wasn't as bad as I had feared. With continued medication to keep battling the infection and more serious food to add strength to the flesh, the gums should start firming up very quickly. But I did confirm one broken tooth, a large upper molar with a bad crack and its nerve exposed. Here was one major cause of pain and infection. Damaged as it was, it was not a good candidate for the root canal that we might otherwise have done. Our only option was to extract it. And so we did. We flushed out the wound and the rest of the mouth with an antiseptic spray, attached Artie to a fluid supply by injection, and waited for him to make the next move.

Artichoke came to after a while and meowed for something. It was too soon for him to eat, which we were sure was what he wanted, so we kept him in suspense for about four hours until we were sure that the effects of the anesthetic had sufficiently worn off. Then we obliged him with a small bowl of water and a dab of baby food, both of which he lapped up with gusto. The breath odor was unbelievably improved; it was like baby's breath. I called Jeff. "Artie's fine. You can pick him up anytime tomorrow."

He stopped by the next day after work. I sent him and Artie off with instructions to go on with the antibiotics but to let me see the cat in five days to check on the extraction. Sunday at my house would be fine. Meantime, he and Mary should start easing Artie into a normal diet of regular cat food.

Later that week, coincidentally, a new patient with a similar complaint was referred to me. The client, Randy Siever, came in with Cigar, a frisky and muscular Havana Brown whose breath could probably have lit cigars but whose mouth was exceptionally clean.

But mixed with the smell of moist cat food, which is not my idea of a treat but is a perfectly normal smell, was the odor of . . . something else. A powerful lot of it.

"Hmmm," I said, running my hands over the cat's muscular young body. "What's the story with these nice clean teeth?"

"Well, he's had this bad breath for a while," said Randy. "I take him to my local vet who looks in his mouth and says, 'This cat needs dentistry. Look, he says—here is plaque that's going right into the gums.' So I look, and I see grungy teeth and some redness of the gums, and I say, okay, do what you have to do. So I leave the cat overnight because he has to be anesthetized for cleaning, and I pick him up the next day. And his breath still smells bad. Maybe a little better, but still bad."

It certainly was. I was beginning to suspect an old and far too familiar acquaintance as the culprit here.

I took Cigar's temperature. Normal would have been 101 to 102 degrees F; his was 103.2. Other than that, and his halitosis, he seemed to be quite a healthy young fellow.

I inspected the mouth again, more thoroughly this time. The teeth were indeed as nice and clean as they could be, and I could see no inflammation of the gums. But I did see a little black spot in the throat, a little black spot that shouldn't have been there. I examined it through an illuminated magnifier. That little black spot turned out to be the eye of a needle with a black thread in it; and further examination revealed that the black thread went right down into the gut.

Same old story. Seems like they'd rather try to swallow a needle than almost anything.

Cigar had swallowed this object in two stages: first, the needle, which lodged in his throat; next, the thread that, still tethered to the needle, had gone clear down to the intestines and gotten locked in. And there it had caused an infection which, in its turn, had produced the bad odor exuding from Cigar's mouth.

Well, everything came out all right, and I was glad of Randy's visit. Many cat owners ignore the need to take care of their cats' teeth and gums, but it's even more important that they be alert to anything in the slightest degree abnormal about their cats' behavior or odor. Monumental bad breath, for example, may signal more than gingivitis or a mouth abscess: it may be a symptom of gastritis, kidney disease or an abscess deep inside.

Randy and Cigar went home happy. Artichoke came back for his five-day checkup. Already, he was a different cat. Gone was the pain and the terrible odor; back was the appetite he once had known, now being whetted by a balanced diet of canned cat food. Soon we'd get him onto dry chow to help keep those teeth clean and in working order.

Could he be starting to fill out so soon? It seemed to me he was. Altogether, he was a happier, friendlier, much nicer cat . . . just the way he should have been always.

We set up a plan for the next appointment and regular checkups.

To my surprise, Jeff and Mary unexpectedly showed up on their horses at my house one summer weekend some time before Artie was due for his first follow-up appointment.

"This isn't for Artie's checkup," Jeff said as they dismounted. "In a way it's ours, I guess." He reached into his saddlebag. "We have something to show you."

"Not Artie?"

At first sight, I thought it really wasn't.

"Yes, it's Artie." Jeff beamed like a proud father. "So long as he felt like taking a ride, we thought you might like to see how he's doing."

I took the cat in my arms and rubbed noses with him. His breath was as sweet as a cat's can be, and he'd gained about two pounds.

"I'm so pleased," I said sincerely. "Now, I have this little tooth-cleaning kit that came in the mail, and I think you might enjoy introducing Artie—"

"No, thank you!" they said in unison.

"All right, then, same time next year," I said.

CHAPTER FIFTEEN

Blue Eyes, Stud Tails *and* Jellicle Genes

Jellicle Cats are black and white,
Jellicle Cats are rather small;
Jellicle Cats are merry and bright,
And pleasant to hear when they caterwaul.

PLEASANT TO HEAR? . . . " Be that as it may—and I've never heard a caterwaul I've really liked—what in the world is a Jellicle cat? And what kind of name is that?

The name is a creation of T.S. Eliot, who wrote exuberantly about all manner of excellent felines in *Old Possum's Book of Practical Cats*. And thanks to the musical "Cats," based on his work, the world knows that Jellicle Cats come out at night and dance by the light of the moon. Fine—but all cats do that. Yet Jellicles are actually dressed for the ball.

The poet's fancy is a tuxedo cat—black and white, merry if not always notably bright, and sometimes more of a moderate to large size than rather small. His claim to fame is that he is actually a mutated descendant of the ancestors of the magical Mr. Mistoffelees, the cat who—according to Eliot—was supposedly quiet and small and black from his ears to the tip of his tail.

As we see by ancient art works, the earliest cats known were tabbies in various dark shadings. In time, the tabby pattern mutated in many different directions, producing, among other things, the non-tabby solid black color of Mr. Mistoffelees. At some later date, the solid black coat underwent a gene mutation that resulted in a spotted or blotched coat with black usually predominant but with areas of white: the tuxedo, or Jellicle, look.

Gene mutations and little blips or accidents or inherited anomalies of multifarious sorts occurring throughout the ages have resulted in a cat population of infinite variety—coats of many colors, defects of many kinds.

I was thinking of this as I watched my new associate handling our new patient.

Dr. Ron Smith had joined my staff right after graduation from veterinary school. He was in the examination room with me when Mrs. Ayers and her two young daughters brought in their cat, Bruce, for a preliminary examination. They'd had him since he was a kitten, but this was their first visit to my office. They told me that Bruce, a lively little tortoiseshell, was five months old, and they wanted to have him altered before he got to be a bigger boy. I don't usually like to have that many people in the room with me when I first examine a cat, but Mrs. Ayers wanted the two little girls to have a learning experience.

As it turned out, we all did.

I had Ron put the cat down on the table and have first tickle with him, and I watched the young doctor stroke the cheeks and chin with a gentle touch.

Bruce was a fine specimen of a tortie, a blended tapestry of black, orange and cream—a calico cat, as Mrs. Ayers fondly suggested.

"Close, but not quite," I said. "The calico has more white than cream and more red than orange. Anyway, we're not going to be able to castrate this cat."

Gasps of surprise and dismay. Dr. Smith looked skeptical.

"Why not?" This was Mrs. Ayers. "What's the problem?"

"Not a problem, really. Only that Bruce is a female, not a male, and we will have to spay her instead."

I could see an amazed look on Ron's face from the corner of my eye. The Ayers ladies murmured their surprise. "Well!" said Mrs. Ayers. "I imagine that what has to be done has to be done anyway. Spay her, of course. But she'll always be Bruce to me. I couldn't think of calling her anything else. It's going to be difficult even getting used to thinking of her as a female!"

"Oh, Mom!" said the littlest girl. "She's Brucie."

"And she's still only a baby," said the bigger one.

When all our callers had left, except Brucie, Dr. Ron Smith said to me: "You must have a hidden mirror or something. How did you know this was a female cat without even looking at the genitalia?"

I love to pull this on the young and innocent. As Pawline's friends will recall, she is a tortoiseshell tabby, too, and the Gardners were also surprised when I told them her sex. But just to be sure this wasn't a once-in-a-lifetime exception, I took a quick peek at my new guest. Brucie it was.

I told Ron: "I've probably examined at least ten thousand cats since becoming a veterinarian, and I've never seen a male tortoiseshell. I know they exist, but they are very rare. And they are almost always sterile."

It seems fantastic, but that's the genes at work. Many minor, and some major, malformations are genetic. Somewhere along the line, little accidents occur and perpetuate themselves or are deliberately perpetuated by breeders. Sometimes the effect is attractive; sometimes it is not. It is seldom useful. Defects in hearing among blue-eyed White Persians and poor vision in some Siamese cats are ill-chosen gifts from their ancestors. So is the distinguishing feature of the Manx cat—its remarkable lack of a tail. Just as some genetic problems are associated with pigmentation or the senses, so are some problems associated with the spinal cord and vertebral column.

The Manx cat can be subject to inherited spina bifida, a condition in which the vertebrae fail to close normally. In the case of a surviving, healthy Manx, the defective gene causes a deformity of the tail— specifically, a very stumpy little residual tail or no tail at all. These cats are fine and sturdy animals. Occasionally, however, unless other genes modify or override the defect, Manx kittens may be afflicted with spines that are seriously incomplete, and in such cases, the kitties are at risk of dying before birth or not long afterwards.

A dog with a docked tail is not unusual, but tailless cats are uncommon enough that they may unwittingly make trouble. They are still not frequently seen, unless you vacation on the Isle of Man or go to a lot of cat shows, but years ago, they were so rare in this country that some people simply didn't believe in them.

The Manx is a nice-looking cat, with the possible exception of its abrupt rear end—which its owners regard as an amusing and endearing feature. It comes in all colors and combinations of colors and makes a delightful pet for people who don't mind owning an animal whose striking feature is its deformity.

Milan Greer, an old client of mine and the breeder who gave my daughter Leslie her aristocratic Abyssinian, told me that at one time, he used to breed and sell Manx cats with some success. He had especially liked the pure white Manx because it looked like a large white bunny rabbit, and apparently quite a number of clients had admired it too.

But not everyone approved of either Milan or the cats, and Milan was obliged to change his ways because of some problems with a disgruntled neighbor. She had always found fault with him for every possible reason, the basic one probably being that she simply didn't want a cattery next door even though it was quiet and impeccably clean. So one day she reported him to the ASPCA for selling cats without tails. He was cutting the tails off, she charged, and selling the cats as rare breeds.

The ASPCA knew Milan Greer by reputation as a distinguished and honorable breeder, one of the most famous in the New York area. Nonetheless—and rightly—they wasted no time in getting over to his establishment to conduct a thorough search and investigation. They inspected Milan's breeding Manxes and their kittens, recognizing them instantly as the genuine article; they questioned his staff and some of his other neighbors, and they talked to his Manx-buying clients. And they found that there was absolutely no basis for the accusation. It had simply been, they agreed, the complaint of a crank.

Now it's possible that the woman had made a genuine mistake. The absence of a tail in a particular cat may not be because it's a Manx but because it had a run-in with a buzz saw or a cat abuser. With tailless cats, it's unwise to leap to a conclusion in either direction.

Well, Milan was vindicated, but he also wanted to end the episode without any loose ends. There was no point in trying to take action against the crank, he decided, but he would stop breeding the Manx. He didn't want the controversy, didn't need the annoyance of ill-founded complaints; didn't want any more hassle. So he sold out his Manx stock, and that was that.

The Manx is a truly classic example of a deformed mutant that earns love by its lovability. So is the cat of many toes.

Standard-issue cats have five toes per foot; polydactyl cats have six or more. Some of them are as dainty and graceful as they can be. Others appear to be shuffling around in ludicrously oversized bedroom slippers. I had a multitoed cat myself once, as a teenager, and one of my young cousins amused herself by saying to me, several times too often, "Ha, ha, ha! Your cat has army boots!" Not funny. I always thought they looked more like boxing gloves. Truth is, an extra toe or two may be an oddity, but usually a harmless one—except for all the ingrowing toenails to which they are prone. For myself, I loved those mighty mitts.

I don't think anybody breeds polydactyls deliberately, nor does anybody get excited about their mini-peculiarity. But the cat lovers of America are in a swivet about a controversial little feline called the Munchkin, a mutant that is now being bred for its mutation: stubby legs. Not only are Munchkins' legs much shorter than those of a normal cat, but their front legs are only half the length of their rear legs. As many a cat fancier has observed, they always look like they're walking downhill.

Opinions of these quaint kitties range from, "Oh, they're so cute!" to "It's a freak! A pitiful, deformed freak!" They're also still rare enough to command a high price among people who have everything. Critics of the breed suggest that Munchkins are likely to have problems, such as arthritis and ailments of the back, leg and hip. But we don't know that yet; they haven't been around long enough. I myself think that they are sweet but freakish, and I'm not very happy with the idea of designer cats.

Getting away from deformities, there are other conditions that tend to show up in some cats more than in others. These may be considered congenital defects or inherited predispositions. I can't say that I can always tell the difference. But one oddity that comes to mind is the case of Mrs. Dora Richmond's Birman.

Mrs. Richmond had two Birman cats, one male and one female. When we met, she had just recently moved from California to New York into an apartment with a screened-in terrace. The Birman cat, incidentally, is a beautiful Southeast Asian with a round head and blue eyes, fur short around the face but long and silky on the body. Bill Bailey Birman, as I came to know the male—Pearl Bailey Birman being his female companion—was a commanding presence with a golden coat, white paws and a dusky tail. His only visible imperfection was his running eye.

Bill Bailey had always had a problem with his right eye. For as long as Mrs. Richmond had had him, he had rubbed at it, and it had teared to some degree. But it had never been too much of an annoyance, and Mrs. Richmond didn't pay too much attention to it. She and her cats had made regular visits to her California veterinarian, and from time to time, he had given her a little eye medicine for Bill Bailey but had never made much of his condition. But after Mrs. Richmond moved to New York, something changed, and Bill started rubbing that right eye constantly.

It was Mrs. Richmond's regular routine to leave the cats out on the terrace whenever she left the apartment during the day. When she noticed Bill's excessive fussing with his eye, she thought something must have blown into it, perhaps a piece of soot. She brought him to my office for an eye examination, and I found his right eye to be quite inflamed.

She was right about the soot. There was a piece of it buried in the conjunctiva. I stained the eye with fluorescein, a fluorescent vegetable dye, to see if there were any lacerations to the cornea. The way the fluorescein works is that, when the eye is examined in a darkened room with a bright light, the dye will fluoresce and invade the laceration of the scratch or any type of abnormality of the cornea.

Fortunately, there was no external damage to the cornea, and I easily removed the piece of soot that was embedded in the conjunctiva. But during the examination, I found that the Birman had a dermoid cyst on his cornea—"dermoid" having to do with skin and skin derivatives. This little abnormality was something he had to have been born with, and it had become increasingly irritating. The cyst had tiny eyelash-type hairs growing out of it, pushing through the cornea, and it must have been a major nuisance for mild-mannered Bill Bailey.

I mentioned this to Mrs. Richmond, wondering why it had not been noticed before.

"I did notice something," she said. "But my vet didn't say anything about it, and I thought it was just a pimple. I didn't think twice about it. Now that you mention it, though, I do believe it has been getting bigger. But it's still just a pimple sort of thing, isn't it?"

"Not really," I said. "It's actually a little hairy tumor, not something that he wants to keep. We should get rid of it before it covers any more of the eye and interferes with his vision."

We made a date for surgery. I did a superficial keratectomy, which is simply the removal of a layer of the cornea including the cyst, and the eye problem was solved. Bill Bailey went home, Pearl was very glad to see him, and in a few weeks the eye was back to normal.

The Rodriguez cats were a more complicated story.

Mrs. Rodriguez owned two cats, one a creamy gray Persian male and the other a female Chocolate-point Siamese. Both cats were super-friendly toward all visitors and super-affectionate with each other. They cuddled together, slept together, ate out of the same bowls and apparently could not bear to be apart. This was intriguing. I have often encountered such a symbiotic relationship between two Siamese cats, but hardly ever with a Siamese and a Persian.

Because of their closeness, Mrs. Rodriguez thought that I ought to see them together. Being a recent arrival from Chile with a heavy Spanish accent, Mrs. Rodriguez was a little bit difficult for me to understand. I did gather, though, that both cats had been neutered and were never out of each other's sight.

What bothered their owner was that the Siamese female was constantly licking the topside of the Persian's tail near the base. This, she thought, was a repellent habit that was not only causing a problem for the male but was actually *caused by* an existing problem in the tail. There was something wrong there, and the female was making it worse.

The upper portion of the tail near the body had been licked almost clean of hair and looked inflamed and infected. There was a discharge and a noxious odor coming from the area, which was why the Siamese was so diligently licking at it. I can't say that she was attracted in the sense of enjoying what she was doing, but she knew a licking job when she saw it and smelled it, and she was doing that job. As for Mrs. Rodriguez, she thought something terrible had happened to the tail and would get even more terrible without any treatment.

I told her that the Persian had a condition called stud tail.

Although I didn't admit to my ignorance, I didn't and I still don't know why it is called stud tail. I think it may be because it primarily affects unneutered males—but the cat in front of me was neutered. Just another mystery of life, I suppose.

There are sebaceous glands on the top of the tail, which sometimes become hyperactive. When this happens, a waxy or oily material is discharged from the glands at the base of the tail, and ordinarily the secretion can be controlled by a safe shampoo. But this had gone too far for that, and now both cats had to be reckoned with. The light-colored Persian was actually stained in the area of the discharge and was clearly infected; the Siamese had gotten addicted to her nurse-attendant duties and was likely to be puzzled by a sudden change in routine.

With this in mind, I cleaned up the tail, treated it with an antibiotic ointment and put a heavy bandage on a good portion of the damaged appendage. It was no longer available to be licked by the Siamese. And so, everybody home, case closed.

But no.

Almost immediately, the Siamese found a substitute for the Persian tail. She got into Mrs. Rodriguez's clothes closet and chewed a big piece of that lady's Paris-made knitted wool shawl. Then she found a sweater and sucked it. Next she was nibbling and sucking and slurping on a pair of wool gloves.

"This is intolerable!" said Mrs. Rodriguez. "How are we going to stop this maddening situation? I love my cats, but it's getting to the point where if we can't cure this and stop them, I'll have to get rid of them!"

"Them"? That seemed harsh. The Persian wasn't doing anything wrong. His tail was still in a sling, though healing nicely, and the Siamese wasn't going anywhere near it.

"I think she has gone sick in the head," Mrs. Rodriguez added.

"No, I really don't think so," I said.

Actually, I found the situation very interesting. Some breeds, especially Siamese and Burmese cats—as distinct from Birmans—have a predilection for wool sucking or chewing of various fabrics, and this little Siamese was one of those cats. Her behavior was not uncommon. The cause is unknown, and there's no specific treatment, but it did seem to me that the perpetrator in this case had substituted one obsession for another. No stud tail? Try wool instead.

I advised Mrs. Rodriguez to keep all the doors closed within the apartment. The cats could only roam in the kitchen, a small bathroom and in the long hallway, therefore the Siamese was not exposed to any wool or other fabric. We gave our client some catnip to ration out to the Siamese twice a day, and a sample package of oatgrass seeds that would grow into grass for the cat to chew on whenever compulsion struck. Mrs. Rodriguez was able to cultivate it right in her own kitchen in a little pot, and when she needed refills, she bought them at her local pet shop. Soon she reported that the combination of catnip and oatgrass was having a salutary effect on the cat.

I should interject here that a little grass goes a long way, and when I say grass, I mean the greenery that grows legitimately in yards and in the wild. Most cats of my acquaintance like to chew on grass and even swallow some. But green stuff—vegetable matter—is not a dietary requirement for cats, and they can't digest much of it. Often it comes up shortly after going down, sometimes bringing with it hairballs-in-the-making. "Cleaning out the digestive system" is what we veterinarians call this process, and although the resultant deposit on the hall rug is unpleasant for the cat owner, it is not a problem for the cat nor a symptom of a digestive disorder. (If hairballs are a factor, a more practical solution is a store-bought and rather tasty emulsion generally known as "hairball remedy," essentially a malt and petrolatum concoction now available in designer flavors.)

Certainly the salad greens for the Siamese were a success. She still loved her Persian, but she stopped yearning for his tail or any suckable substitute.

It took about three months for the Persian's tail to heal completely. To be absolutely sure that the situation was under control, we kept his bandage on for quite a while longer and continued to have all interior doors closed. Mrs. Rodriguez was incredibly patient. She really did love those cats.

After six months, the cycle was broken. No more stud tail, no more sucking. Mrs. Rodriguez let both of the cats into her bedroom again, where they curled up on the bed and snuggled with each other as in the days before the obsession began.

Some time during that period, a new client came in with an old dog and a new question—a new question for her, but one that is often asked by breeders or by teachers at a veterinary school:

"If I mate my white cat with another white cat, will we get white kittens?"

And I had to answer: "Who knows? Unless you have the family tree of both of those white cats, you can't know what you're going to get. As we say in the veterinary business, a white cat is a cat in disguise."

She did mate them. And when the babies came, there was one white kitten with a splash of yellow and four other cats in a combination of thirteen other colors.

And that is a revealing family portrait indeed.

CHAPTER SIXTEEN

How Well Do Cats Hear

and

Why Don't They Listen?

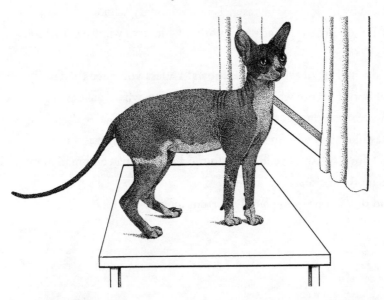

WILLIAM DOUGLAS OWNED an exceptionally intelligent cat, or so he thought. Actually, Willie the cat was bright, but he wasn't quite the genius Mr. Douglas thought him to be. The thing about Willie was, he really looked intimidatingly clever.

He was a brown and white Sphynx with large golden eyes and enor-

mous ears the size of satellite dishes. The friends who had given him
to Mr. Douglas when the cat was six months old had named him Willie
after his new master, thinking it highly amusing that the man and the
cat were both bald. In fact, Mr. Douglas had a truly shining dome,
but the four-legged Willie wasn't really bald at all. Sphynxes—not
Egyptian cats, as the name might suggest, but Canadian in origin—
are often described as hairless cats because they appear to be almost
totally bare. Looking at them, you see a rather grotesque little creature with every line and wrinkle of its body exposed, and the human reaction is generally rather negative. But the cat does have hair, so short
over most of the body that it's virtually invisible except for the pat-
terning, and to the touch it feels like an Ultrasuede hot-water bottle. To
me, Willie looks less like a Willie than an E.T., a very affectionate and
sociable E.T., and either because or in spite of his oddness, I find him
very endearing.

The main reason Mr. Douglas's friends had given him the cat was
that they felt he needed a lively but not too demanding animal companion. They had chosen the Sphynx because Douglas was allergic to
cats, even though he rather liked them, and his friends were under
the impression that a practically hairless cat was a non-allergenic form
of feline.

This was a mistake. People who are allergic to cats are not immune
to the Sphynx. The hair of the cat is not the problem.

Nor is the allergic reaction caused by the cat's dander, as once
thought, although the dead skin constantly sloughing off is a contrib-
utory factor. The allergen is secreted in the cat's saliva and from the cat's
skin. So if you had a skinless cat that never washed itself, you might
be onto something.

I am embarking on this little dander detour here because so many
people are allergic to cats and many of them think the Sphynx is the answer to the sneezy cat-lover's prayer. I had to explain all this to Mr.
Douglas when he first brought Willie in for vaccinations and wondered
why his own eyes were so itchy. I gave him a spray that would reduce

the shedding of the dander, and I suggested that he use this, or plain club soda, three times a week to keep down the dust on Willie. That would help, but more effective would be a weekly bath, a prospect that did not appeal to Mr. Douglas and a reality that appealed even less to Willie.

But Mr. Douglas tried valiantly, and one way or another, he kept Willie sprayed down at least a couple of times a week and bathed whenever he could find a helping hand among his widowed lady friends. All these efforts seemed to help, otherwise William and Willie would have had to part.

But Willie was too special for William to let him go.

In the opinion of Mr. Douglas and his friends, Willie was an exceptionally responsive cat. They used to comment that Willie knew his name and would actually come when called, and they thought this was a sign of markedly superior intelligence. Visitors would say, "What a smart cat you have!" And of course Mr. Douglas was very happy about this and loved the compliments.

I was a little muted in my enthusiasm. Of course a cat knows the sound of its name and when it's being called, and the approximate nature of the call. "Dinner, darling Willie!" is one thing. "Get outta here, Willie, you rotten hairball!" is something else. Believe me, they know the difference. And of course Mr. Douglas didn't address Willie in anything other than dulcet tones. So I really didn't think Willie was a towering intellect.

One day I received a call from Mr. Douglas about Willie. He said that for about two months, Willie had been acting sort of sluggish, not really sick but just sluggish, and he had almost stopped responding to his name when he was called. Mr. Douglas didn't know if Willie had forgotten his name or if he was sick or what was the matter.

"He doesn't answer to his name!" I exclaimed. But this was Willie's big schtick! Forgotten it? I didn't think so.

So we arranged for an examination.

Mr. Douglas arrived and took Willie out of his carrying case. I could see at once that something wasn't right.

Willie shook his head and scratched an ear.

"Hello, Willie!" I said loudly.

He peered at me uncertainly.

"Boo!" I clapped my hands.

No reaction. But when I tickled his tummy he squirmed appreciatively. I wouldn't say that he was unresponsive.

"You say he's sluggish," I remarked. "Any problem with his coordination? Loss of balance, walking a crooked line, falling off the furniture?"

"Good heavens, no," said Mr. Douglas. "He's not a drinking cat, you know." And he laughed immoderately.

"Huh. Wouldn't be the first," I said. "But I believe we'll find he hasn't been hearing well. And when there's a hearing problem there's often a corresponding ataxia. That is, his balance could be affected. But let's take a look at this."

"This" was Willie's head. There was something awfully odd about its size and shape.

"A hearing problem?" Mr. Douglas said, wonderingly. I examined Willie's head, close-up. The first off-key thing I had noticed was unmistakable. "Do you often see him shaking his head or scratching his ears? Or just twitching his ears?"

"Well, no, not particularly."

The cat's left ear was swollen to about four times normal size. He flinched when I touched it. The other was also inflamed. Not nearly so badly, but it was starting to look infected.

"Has he been fighting lately?"

Mr. Douglas was scandalized. "Of course not!"

"I think his problem is in his ears," I said mildly. "See the swelling now?" I was trying not to be judgmental, but I was thinking, You'd have to be blind not to have noticed this. It continues to astound me that people who are crazy about their cats don't seem to notice some of their most alarming symptoms. What could be more obvious than a lopsided, swollen head?

"Oh, I didn't see that, I didn't see that," Mr. Douglas moaned guiltily. "His head's all out of shape. Why? I don't understand why. You say he can't hear?"

"I doubt if he can hear very much. He has a bad infection in this one ear, possibly in both. I suspect a foreign body here. Probably many foreign bodies."

I reached for my otoscope and a swab.

Mr. Douglas was murmuring something about it being impossible for Willie to have any kind of infection, but it's never impossible. I'd seen enough of Willie to know that he wasn't congenitally deaf, and he wasn't old enough to be losing his hearing naturally. Furthermore, I knew these symptoms well, and I knew this infection was advanced. If we didn't attend to it at once, he might suffer permanent damage.

A cat's hearing is one of its most valuable attributes. Deaf cats can make astounding adjustments to the absence or loss of a sense so superb that it sometimes seems like a sixth sense. But, precisely because the sense is so acute, for a cat to lose its hearing is something like losing a vital connection with its natural world. The high-pitched squeaking of a mouse, the rustling of a leaf outside, a stealthy footfall, a distant bark, the soft little sucking sound of a refrigerator door being opened one floor down and three rooms away, these are sounds that cats can hear and we cannot.

I examined Willie's ear canal with the otoscope. It was, in the jargon of the veterinary trade, a mess. Here they were, my old friends *Otodectes cynotis*, the most common cause of ear disorders in dogs as well as cats. The canal was practically occluded with dark wax and debris. Moistening the cotton swab with mineral oil, I took a sample of the ear contents and turned it over to my assistant Penelope to prepare a slide for the microscope. It was no wonder Willie didn't answer to his name; the left ear was so clogged with exudate, it was a wonder he could hear anything at all.

Willie gave me a sidelong glance and tried to scratch his swollen ear as I looked into the other one with the otoscope.

We've all seen cats staring intently into space as if looking at a ghost we cannot see. But they're far more likely to be listening to a sound we cannot hear. Their hearing range is up to two octaves higher than the highest note detectable by the human ear, and about half an octave higher than the highest note a dog can hear. Put another way, humans can hear sounds up to the limit of twenty kilohertz; cats can hear sounds as high as sixty kilohertz.

It is true that when they're gazing at the unseen they may not actually be hearing anything at all. At times they have this look of being lost in contemplation of some cosmic truth, and perhaps they are. They sit there in their neat little pose, unmoving, tails wrapped around their toes, gazing unblinkingly at infinity and looking dauntingly superior. We think: *Something must be going through those minds.* Yes, something is. Little wisps of cloud pass idly between those excellent ears, touching lightly upon kitty knowledge of can-opener sounds and creature comforts. Why should anything else be going on? It's not that they're dumb; far from it. They're too smart to waste effort on excess thought.

And then there are times when cats, like humans, simply don't hear anything they don't want to hear. They are deliberately oblivious; they are stubborn. They don't know any better? Sure they do. "Come here for your bath, Fluffy!" Doesn't come. "Get off the dining room table!" Sits there, washing whiskers. "Here's your nice dinner!" Isn't in the mood for Primetime Senior Care Maintenance Diet tonight. Stares at the television, where several tap-dancing cats are singing songs about much friskier food.

Willie would not have been doing much of that lately.

The right ear was going to be fine once we'd cleaned it up. The swollen left ear, however, would require more drastic measures.

I looked at the slide under the microscope. The nasty little things were crawling all over it, wading through the waxy debris with their tiny little legs, waving their tiny little tentacles. I made a face and a sound like Yuck. I've seen millions of these little critters, but they always give me the creeps. It's odd, how some of the tiniest of nature's creatures can be so repellent.

Mr. Douglas said anxiously, "What is it? What's the matter?"

"Ear mites," I said. "Parasites. An earful of them. This one ear is really bad, and some of these creatures have migrated to the other ear as they tend to do. They live by piercing the skin inside the ear and sucking the lymph. This causes irritation and itching. Willie's irritated, all right, and he's itching, and there's a crust forming inside the ear. But with this left ear, this balloon here, he probably did some extra damage to himself. Most likely, he shook his head to get rid of the itching and hit it against something. So he wound up with bleeding under the skin—a hematoma—which made the whole ear swell and balloon out like well, like a small balloon. And that's going to require surgery."

"It's hard to believe that you have to operate for ear mites," Mr. Douglas said. But he didn't argue.

"It's not just the ear mites," I said. "If they'd been caught earlier, we could have cleaned them out with a few treatments of ear drops. It's what they do that's dangerous. Cat gets irritated, infected, scratches itself to pieces, whacks its head and winds up with hematomas. So the first thing we do is flush out those ears and get rid of the little creeps. I'd suggest that you leave him here for us to clean him up and operate. We can do the surgery in the morning, and you can pick him up tomorrow night. How's that?"

It was fine with Mr. Douglas. In the morning, we tranquilized Willie to clean out his ears and followed up with a general anesthetic for surgery on the swollen ear. Penelope and I drained the bloody fluid out of the ear, inserted a drain to draw off the residue and put a mild but firm pressure badge over the area of the operation. This had to be done at the start of the healing process, otherwise the magnificent ear would droop down and fold over like the ear of a Scottish Fold—a totally different breed of cat.

We put Willie on an antibiotic to control the bacterial infection caused by the ear mites and started him on a series of injections to destroy any remaining parasites. Mr. Douglas picked him up and went home happily, promising to be very disciplined about Willie's medication.

A little to my surprise, he was as diligent as he had promised to be. In about three weeks, all traces of the ear mites were gone, and Willie's ears were standing up like sentinels.

Shortly thereafter, Willie started responding to his name.

Mr. Douglas telephoned me in great excitement.

"He comes when I call!" he chirped. "He comes even when I don't call! He hears when I put the dry cat food in his bowl. He comes when I use the electric can opener, even when it isn't for him. He hears my footsteps when I come home, and when I get to the door, he's sitting there waiting to greet me. He races to the window and chatters when he hears birds chirping . . ."

I smiled as I listened to the litany of Willie's wonders. He was back to being a normal cat. I was happy for him and his owner . . . who was still talking.

"He's clever, isn't he?" said Mr. Douglas proudly.

"Very clever, Mr. Douglas," I said gravely.

And then, during the next few weeks, or perhaps it was months, funny things started to happen. Mr. Douglas was combing his few remaining hairs one day when he chanced to run his thumb over the teeth of his comb, making a little prrrrrrrrp! sound. Willie was with him, and Willie reeled back with a sick look on his face and gagged. Mr. Douglas did it again, and so did Willie. It was like chalk on a blackboard, Mr. Douglas explained.

Next, Mr. Douglas caught a little cold and developed a high-pitched sneeze. Each time he sneezed, Willie meowed. It was sneeze-meow-sneeze-meow all day long for about a week. When that was over, Mr. Douglas felt ready for an evening of music with guests. One of his lady friends sat down at the piano, tinkled the keys, and sang in a glass-shattering soprano. Willie opened his mouth in an impolite screech of disapproval. Both pianist and critic did encores. But when the violinist went to work, Willie was much more discreet. He opened his mouth wide, his jaw worked, but not a sound came out.

"Now, what does that mean?" Mr. Douglas said indignantly. "It there something the matter with his voice?"

"Why, it's a sign of appreciation," I lied. "It's the silent meow. You just couldn't hear him, but he was meowing along with the music, at a much higher pitch."

"Oh." His owner was gratified. "The silent meow. I like that."

I did, too. Appreciative Willie was reaching a kilohertz high that was no doubt heard by all the neighborhood cats, and I don't think that what he was saying was complimentary to the fiddler. Silent meows are really quite common. So are reactions to sounds that individual cats find disturbing. A writer friend of mine, for instance, gets instant writer's block when his adopted alley cat, Boots, comes up behind him and makes hideous retching sounds as the fingers tap away at the keyboard. What a way to make a living. Everybody an editor, even the cat.

I concluded my conversation with Mr. Douglas by assuring him that Willie's hearing was excellent and so were his vocal cords. He was just expressing himself.

"But then, you see," I added, "as I've always said, Willie is an exceptionally clever cat."

CHAPTER SEVENTEEN

The Cat
Who Couldn't See
in the Dark

FLOYD WAS A SWEET BUT SICKLY LOOKING little orange tabby, about two and a half years old when the Ambertons first brought him to the clinic. "Little" is not the usual word for an orange cat. Most of those I've seen, even when ailing, are large, rotund and full of themselves. Floyd was skinny and listless and seemed too weak to walk.

His people were in their early thirties. They were lean and rangy and dressed in biking gear. When they spoke they talked in turns, overlapping, the way many of my client couples do.

I ran my hands over Floyd and felt his ribs. They were much too close to the surface.

"What seems to you to be the problem?" I asked.

"It may be something with his eyes," they said diffidently.

"His eyes!" Of all things. I was tempted to say something like, "Why, can't he see his food?" but said instead, "How's that?"

"Well, he keeps walking into things, as if he can't see them. It started at night, in the dark. You know, sometimes things would go bump in the night, and in the morning, we'd see something knocked over, as if he can't find his way around any more. But cats are supposed to be able to see in the dark."

I waggled my fingers back and forth in front of his lackluster but responsive eyes, and said: "How long has this been going on?"

"Oh, maybe weeks—"

"And only in the dark?"

"Lately, sometimes in the daytime, too, but he doesn't walk around a lot. He doesn't have much energy any more."

Any more? I wondered if he'd ever had much.

"Weeks? . . . " I murmured. "You weren't worried?"

They looked abashed. "Well, yes. We procrastinated. But he suddenly started looking really ill. Not just bumping into stuff, but weak, could hardly walk, could hardly even stand. And he had difficulty breathing."

I could see this for myself. To me, Floyd's situation was serious and urgent.

"Okay, and when did that start?"

"It's just within the last twenty-four hours that he's seemed this bad."

Bumping into the furniture was the least of his problems.

The idea of him stumbling around in the dark was ludicrous. Cats *can* see in the dark. Not in absolute pitch darkness, which is a popular misconception, but in the deep dimness that passes for darkness among humans. In near-dark, their pupils dilate to draw in all the available light that we don't even realize is there. Floyd might possibly be short-sighted, but he wasn't blind. And even if his eyes were a serious problem, his whiskers would help him out. Cats get a lot of help from their whiskers to judge distances at night, and in the daytime, if necessary. Each whisker, from the long muzzle whiskers flanking the nose to the tiny ones above the eyes and on the elbows, acts as an antenna sending messages to the brain as the cat nears an obstruction, brushes past it or even encounters an air current.

Still, his people's concern about his sight was intriguing.

Yet there was nothing wrong with the appearance of his eyes. No cataract, no cloudiness, no damage to the cornea. Possibly something deeper, then.

While this passed through my mind I went on with my hands-on checkup, scanning his ears and mouth and throat, nose and whiskers and tail and legs, feeling him for lumps and swellings, getting ready to ask what I nearly always ask up front and feeling almost sure it would be the crucial question.

"What does he eat?"

"Oh, he eats very much what we eat ourselves—good, wholesome food." I looked at them, and they certainly looked better than Floyd. In fact, for a fleeting moment, they seemed to have an aura about them that said to me, "And see how healthy we are." But his was not the look of a cat accustomed to table scraps.

"So, what does everybody eat?"

Here it was: oatmeal, water, grains, vegetables, rice and fruit.

"His two favorite things," they enthused, "are corn on the cob and cantaloupe. Oh, and he loves grapes. And he gets sunflower oil on his food. And we give him pretzels as a treat. He loves to lick the salt off first and then eat the pretzels."

I could see why he yearned for salt. It was the closest thing to a meaty protein taste that he could put in his mouth. None of what he was eating was bad for him; it simply lacked what was necessary for animal well-being—necessary for his survival.

"You are vegetarians?" I said politely.

"Yes, yes, of course!"

"Yes, well, of course, the cat is not." I was really quite put out with them. "Cats are what we call *obligate carnivores*. That means they *must* eat animal tissue. We don't have to; they do. It is absolutely essential to them. They must have meat protein, and plenty of it. Nature simply didn't supply them with a lot of the enzymes needed to produce some of the necessary nutrients that are not found in vegetable matter. A cat could die from a vegetarian diet. How long has he been on it?"

Floyd's people were looking rather stunned.

"Oh, ten or twelve months," the woman stammered. "He was given to us when he was about a year and a half."

"Lucky it wasn't longer," I observed, "or he might not have been with us at all." I don't like to be disagreeable with my clients, but human fads or dietary preferences can be deadly for animals. It is not cute to turn one of nature's hunter/meat eaters into a vegan.

"Actually," I added, "cantaloupe is pretty good for cats, but only as a small part of a well-rounded, protein-centered diet. The only essentials he's been getting are water and fiber."

I asked the Ambertons to sit in the waiting room while my tech Melissa and I gave Floyd as thorough a checkup as we could without getting into exhaustive detail. It didn't seem to me that we had much time to waste. We took his temperature, which was normal, and a blood sample for in-house analysis.

Checking Floyd's eyes with the ophthalmoscope, I found he had the start of retinal degeneration. So he did have something of an eye problem. This would not cause him to bash into the furniture, but it was a not-unexpected indicator of what was ailing him. I listened to his heart. The heart sounds were abnormal; here was another piece of evidence, undoubtedly relating to his breathing problem. I lifted his fragile little body. Of course this fragility was grossly abnormal. The poor guy couldn't walk. He couldn't stand. He was hungry, he was miserable, and he was dangerously undernourished.

In discussing Floyd's case, my colleagues and I found his condition to be a true emergency. Worst was the cardiac problem, and next-worst was that he was too malnourished and weak for us to make all our diagnostic tests. We would have liked to make others, but they would have to wait until he had the strength for them. Meanwhile, on the basis of his diet, his eye problem and his heart symptoms, we made an initial diagnosis of retinal and cardiac disease due to taurine deficiency.

I called in the Ambertons for a consultation.

"Just let me make sure I understand this correctly," I said. "Floyd has not been eating any meat or meat products or commercial cat food, dry or canned?"

"Oh, no!" they said, as if genuinely shocked by the notion.

"We have an emergency on our hands," I said. "A life and death situation. Floyd's diet is killing him."

They stiffened, not wanting to believe.

"Believe me," I said. "Cats need animal tissue to create proteins. They need *fats*—yes, fats, and vitamins and minerals and carbohy-drates. Most of all, they have to have essential amino acids to create those proteins. One of the most essential amino acids for cats—and I mean *vital*—is called taurine. Floyd hasn't been getting any taurine. None at all. And taurine deficiency in cats can cause blindness and heart disease and reproductive problems. That last one's not going to bother Floyd, but his sight and his heart are affected. And, as you've pointed out, he is having difficulty breathing. We'd like to put him into an oxygen tent right away. May we do that?"

They agreed, and we did.

We talked some more.

Taurine, I told them, is an amino acid found in high concentra-tions in meat, fish and shellfish. This was the most basic element lack-ing in their kitty's diet, but not the only one.

"We need to do two things for Floyd right now," I said, "if you want to save him. We have to treat him for his heart condition, and we'll have to give him a taurine supplement. Otherwise we might lose him. And if he rallies, he's got to have a complete change of diet."

Watching their changing expressions, I was sorry for them. Clearly they wanted to save him. Clearly they weren't too thrilled about the change of diet. And clearly they realized the seriousness of the situation. What they said was, "Do anything you think is right."

"The diet shouldn't be a problem," I said gently, now that I had made my point. "You don't have to get anything special for him but a good-quality commercial cat food. Look at the label, at the ingredient list. Meat-based protein should be high on the list. Don't try dog food; it doesn't work. Dogs have a lower protein requirement, and commercial dog foods do not contain taurine. But cats have to have it."

"If you do save him," Mrs. Amberton said, "he can have caviar."

"I have high hopes," I said, "but you can give me the caviar."

They left then, without Floyd, who was too weak to return home.

We put him in intensive care and did a complete blood chemistry on his blood sample. The plasma taurine concentration was alarmingly low, confirming our analysis.

Luckily, and a little to my surprise, Floyd could still eat on his own. We opened a can of cat food— a completely balanced diet including the requisite taurine—near him as he lay on his sickbed, and his nostrils started to quiver. I can tell you, Prime Entree smells a whole lot better to a cat than oatmeal or rice, and the smell of food is just as important to a cat as its taste.

My tech put some of the food in a bowl, and Floyd leaned right over to vacuum it up. I swear he smacked his lips. Actually, I've never seen a cat as sick as Floyd eat with such gusto and so fast. We had to withhold the rest of the can from him; he was enjoying it too much, and we weren't ready to have him stuff himself after so many months of deprivation.

We started the taurine supplement immediately and kept him on it, maintaining the oxygen while putting him through procedures to remove excess fluids from his body, allow him to breathe more easily and strengthen the heart muscle. And, of course, we fed him nourishing, heavenly kitty food.

In a few days, Floyd was feeling stronger, and his respiration was much improved. All tests confirmed our diagnosis of taurine deficiency—but not as extreme as it had been. Furthermore, he was no longer quite so scrawny an orange cat. His tiny tummy already seemed to be filling out. This guy was going to make it. We sent him home with the Ambertons and a brief note regarding his care and feeding.

In three weeks, he was a different cat. With medication and on the proper diet, Floyd was feeling well, acting frisky and living a normal life. He was no longer falling over the furniture. I checked him out, and he licked my hand. I love it when they do that. It may have been just my salty taste, but I felt that he rather liked me. What was he saying to himself? I wondered. Thank the kitty gods—I'm getting yummy food!

I thought the Ambertons were a little different, too. They were all smiles when I checked out Floyd and pronounced him not only alive but well.

"There, now," I said, pleased. "The diet is everything."

"It's pretty good for us, too," the Ambertons agreed.

I raised an eyebrow.

It turned out that they had modified their own very strict vegetarian fare, and were no longer the most pure of vegetarians. They had actually—gasp!—eaten a meat-flavored vegetable stew, and loved it. *And* a green salad with a little tuna.

I was proud of them. I eat very little meat myself, but I'm not a fanatic—except so far as animals are concerned. Particularly cats.

"That's terrific," I said sincerely. "Keep doing what you're doing with him. Spare the broccoli. Go easy on the brussels sprouts. Eat them yourself. They're good for you. But please—spare the cat."

And now, two years later, he is a nice, well-rounded orange marmalade cat. Even his color is better. His full name, incidentally, is Pink Floyd.

One little footnote: The other day, I was passing one of the neighborhood luncheonettes that serve sandwiches, burgers and coffee, and there at a table in the window were the Ambertons. Both were munching on something in a bun.

Tofuburgers? Somehow I didn't think so.

They looked up, saw me and waved.

I waved back, shamelessly peering at what was on their plates.

Definitely not tofuburger. It looked a whole lot more like the human equivalent of Kitty Prime Entree.

I smiled, and walked back to my clinic.

But I never did get my caviar.

CHAPTER EIGHTEEN

Allergies *and* Uninvited Guests

SOMETIMES A SOLUTION comes right out of the blue. In one case it had to, because, in fact, I never even met the cat. Not then, or ever. Inspiration came to me one summer when the poolwoman was cleaning my pool. She was not a chatty person as a rule, and certainly not one to solicit advice, but on this occasion, she just happened to get talking about her cat. He hadn't seemed happy for about six years, she said; he didn't have fleas, but he apparently did have a chronic itch because he kept scratching himself; and she couldn't figure out what ailed him. She'd had him to four or five vets over the years, and they hadn't been able to come up with the answer either. Otherwise, he seemed healthy but irritable.

I thought this was pretty sad. That cat's been unhappy for about six years, and nobody knows what to do about it!

There could be any number of diagnoses, but I had a thought.

I said, "It sounds like an allergy. What are you feeding him? Does he eat much fish? Fish is a common cause of allergy."

She said, "Yes, he'll eat hardly anything but canned tuna."

Lots of cats are addicted to canned tuna, and many of them have allergic reactions to it. I said, "Eliminate the tuna. See what happens."

What happened, of course, is that the cat raised hell and turned up his nose at the Gourmet Steak and Chicken Stew until driven to eat by sheer hunger, and within three weeks—she told me later—was a different cat. He'd quit scratching, he was better-natured, and he tucked into a wide variety of Kitty Fishless Feasts with never a mutter of rebellion. Best of all, so far as she was concerned, was his contentment. After six years of unnecessary misery, he was at last a happy cat.

I was more than content myself, because my reward for good advice was a free pool cleaning, but I also got to give one of my minidiscourses on the care and feeding of felines. The fact is that fish is not a natural food for cats, and many cats—especially those who get hooked on tuna—can't tolerate it. But lots of cat owners don't know this, and their vets don't always think to tell them.

It occurred to me then that there's a lot more to cat care than a well-balanced program to keep kitty long-lived and svelte, and a lot of things that cat owners wonder about and never think to ask. Like why does a cat itch when there doesn't seem to be a flea or a speck of flea dirt in sight? Because cats can have allergies, too. Besides fish, the allergen could be airborne pollen or vegetable pollen or feathers or hypersensitivity to the bite of a long-gone flea. Or the problem could actually be hypersensitivity to a whole flock of fleas, seen or unseen.

More advice: If you can't figure out why your cat keeps on sneezing or scratching, make a note of its unusual behavior and consult your vet. Felix may have encountered an allergen.

Fleas, however, can be a major and horrible problem well beyond the allergy factor.

Two favorite clients of mine, sisters in their seventies, lived together at the time this story begins in a rambling, many-roomed apartment left to them by their parents.

I had known the McPherson sisters fairly well socially before they became clients, and I knew that after adopting Abigail and Agatha, they were much happier people than when they had been cat-free. The kittens, gift of a friend and sisters themselves, had become more than members of the family. They *were* the family.

The McPhersons loved to play with the cats, throw Ping-Pong balls to them, watch them romp around the house, watch them jump on the couch and play tag around the furniture. They had a great deal of fun with them right from the beginning, which made it all the more surprising that, when they brought in the cats—now a little over a year old—for their general examinations, these sweet women were distraught to the point of tears. They simply couldn't deal with what was happening. They wouldn't have believed it possible.

And they had certainly suffered too long before seeking help. It's odd, but otherwise sensible people can let a bad situation get out of hand until it's almost beyond solution. Part of their inability to take action, I think, is just not realizing that experts can help, and part is simple embarrassment.

The problem? Fleas. A massive infestation, an invasion, a hostile takeover of the entire household by veritable armies of fleas. Fleas were all over the apartment, all over the cats, and the McPherson sisters themselves were bitten up by fleas. I could see the little inflamed marks on them. They had tried all kinds of home remedies, flea sprays and powders and the ever-popular baking soda, and nothing had helped. The infiltration had begun stealthily about six or eight weeks ago, and steadily escalated to the point where they just couldn't stand it. They even dreaded going to bed, knowing they'd wake up with a new plague of itching bites to face a new day of intolerable stress.

As if the flea invasion were not horror enough, they had another problem: Abigail and Agatha were destroying the furnishings, the precious accumulations of many years. They had never clawed their surroundings before, but once they started scratching their flea bites, they seemed to want to scratch everything in sight. Carpets, upholstery, table legs, curtains, pillows, throw rugs—everything was being destroyed. Those relentless claws were dismantling the house. Some of the upholstery pieces literally looked as if they had been shredded . . . which indeed they had.

The McPherson ladies had tried clipping the cats' nails, but that didn't help. They got scratching posts—no improvement. They even tied catnip bags to the scratching posts, as a neighbor had suggested, but Abigail and Agatha still preferred the furniture.

The situation was awful! Frustration level high, furniture in shreds, apartment bursting at the seams with fleas, flea bites for everyone, cats losing hair, cats and ladies losing tempers . . . the McPhersons were at their wits' end.

Describing the situation to me, the sisters were teary-eyed. They loved their cat babies and could scarcely contemplate parting with them, but they were coming to the point where they felt they had no alternative. They admitted that they hadn't done any entertaining for weeks. Even in the neighborhood, they were shy of having people see their tattered clothes and ravaged skin. Friends would invite them to their homes for dinner or cocktails, and they couldn't reciprocate. They were ashamed of their disheveled apartment and dreaded the thought of fleas hopping on visitors.

A real dilemma!

I found it hard to believe that these impeccable ladies, so innocent until now of onslaughts by hordes of vermin, were not exaggerating. But when they blushingly showed me their arms and legs, I saw almost uninterrupted legions of flea bites. The cats themselves were so heavily infested that I could actually see the fleas scampering about without even ruffling their fur. Little runaways skittered around on the examination table and dropped to the floor, running.

"Whoa!" I leapt for the emergency spray.

But there *was* a solution, and a dramatic one. The cats would have to be hospitalized to rid them of fleas. The infestation was so extreme that we'd have to keep them in the clinic and out of the apartment until we had wiped out the last flea. The ladies agreed. Anything to rid their lives of fleas! I told them that we'd immerse the cats in a solution of flea dip.

"You mean bathe them?" one of the sisters said dubiously. "They hate water. We tried to bathe them once and they just went crazy."

"Don't worry," I said. "We'll give them a mild tranquilizer, and I'm sure they won't mind the flea dip at all."

To deal with the other half of their problem—namely, the cats' destructive behavior—I proposed that once the fleas were gone, we declaw Agatha and Abigail. This would save the furniture and keep the peace; and it would not be painful for the cats.

"We've thought about it and read articles," said the elder Miss McPherson, "but surely they are not complete without their claws. It seems a cruel and mutilating thing to do."

"Not at all," I said. "Both my cats are declawed, and that doesn't stop them from climbing trees and chasing squirrels. As a rule, we only do the front claws. They keep the hind ones. And I don't believe they're aware of the difference."

I explained that, when we do the declawing, we give the cats general anesthesia so that they are completely asleep during the operation. They stay in the hospital overnight with bandages on their paws. There is no pain at all. I told them that I had declawed thousands of cats with excellent results. People are uniformly delighted to have their pets returned to them as the wonderful sweethearts they once were, and to have their furniture safe from further assault. It makes for a more tranquil household for all concerned—more affection, less yelling and generally a happier companionship.

But, I added, the decision is not mine to make. I can understand people's feelings on both sides.

The McPhersons were still dubious about declawing. After all, cats were born with claws, and removing them was surely unnatural. But getting rid of the fleas was another story.

Because the infestation was so aggressive, I gave the sisters both flea spray and aerosol flea bombs for every room in their apartment. Ordinarily, spray alone, generously applied and repeated a time or two, would be enough to kill both fleas and eggs, but we had a monster invasion here. Before doing anything else, I explained, they had to vacuum everything thoroughly to remove surface fleas and eggs: the carpets, the closets, the beds, the sofas, the chairs, the bare floors— every nook and cranny. A big job. "Use disposable vacuum bags," I said, "and get rid of them at once." And then they were to spray under beds, sofas and chairs, and along the baseboards of all the rooms in the house. Finally, they were to close the windows, set off the flea bombs, and leave the apartment for four hours.

The bad news was that they would have to do it again in about ten days to two weeks. It takes the eggs anything from two to twelve days to hatch, and we'd have to deliver at least a one-two punch to finish off the adults and all their offspring.

"Oh, I don't know if we can do that," sighed the younger Miss McPherson. "Of course we can," the older said crisply.

Their cats stayed for defleaing and the sisters departed, scratching.

They followed my program to the letter, vacuuming and bombing like veterans. When they returned to their apartment after a four-hour lunch and shopping trip, they could see dead fleas everywhere, even in the bedding. They were amazed at the quantity. And they'd thought they kept such a clean house! And so they did, but fleas don't care. The sisters piled bedding into the washing machine and plugged in the vacuum cleaner again.

Meanwhile, we'd tranquilized and dipped the cats. When they were removed from the little tub, the surface was awash in dead fleas. Towel drying and subsequent combing brought up even more bodies. Just as the McPhersons could scarcely believe the number of fallen fleas in their apartment, so was I astounded at what Abigail and Agatha had yielded. This was the most severe flea infestation I'd seen in years—

but it was not unprecedented. When those little monsters get dug in, they are hell to remove. I'd given out many flea bombs before now.

The McPhersons, with one problem under control, telephoned to say that they had reconsidered about the declawing. They wanted it done, after all. I was a little surprised, but I think perhaps the sight of their tattered furniture in the absence of cats may have had something to do with their change of heart. I told them that their kitties were clearly feeling more comfortable after their bath. They'd stopped scratching, started eating and were purring even as we spoke. We'd let them rest for a couple of days before surgery, I said, to recover from one procedure before hitting them with another.

After having Agatha and Abigail fast for a night, we gave them a general anesthetic the morning of the surgery, then washed and disinfected the claw area. Although declawing is a safe and simple operation, it nevertheless *is* an operation, and it is always done under sterile conditions. I told the McPhersons, when they came to take the kitties home, that the cats might walk a little gingerly at first, but any minor discomfort would soon disappear. They were to use only shredded newspaper in the litter box for seven days while the paws were healing, and then bring the kitties back to me to get the bandages removed.

Back they came, poor little kitties, not only to have their stitches removed but—just to make sure—have another flea bath. And while the cats were with me once again, the sisters might as well take another crack at flea-bombing the apartment. Take no prisoners! we agreed. This might seem like overkill, but there's no such thing as overkilling an attack force of fleas.

The next day the cats went home, a little nervous from so much unaccustomed activity, but pain-free, flea-free and coats shining. The McPhersons called a few days later to say how pleased they were. Abigail and Agatha were happy, walking normally and jumping easily onto dressing tables and countertops. And when they found they could no longer claw the furniture, they gave up trying and just stroked it instead.

So things returned to normal. No more itching and scratching, no more reupholstering of furniture, and guests once again being unashamedly and graciously entertained.

You would think that, after that, it would be possible for me to take a holiday from fleas. But it was not to be. The ubiquitous little creatures can turn up everywhere.

Paddling in the surf on a Florida vacation, my wife and I got talking to a couple paddling around near us. They mentioned that they lived on Sutton Place in New York City, which is right around the corner from my clinic. We all agreed it was one small world. They often walked up Fifty-second Street, they said, and added how much they liked the flower boxes in the clinic windows.

We introduced ourselves: Jane and Howard Padwee, George and Barbara Atkins.

"Now that we know you as the veterinarian with the window boxes," said Barbara Atkins, "I'd like to tell you about our cat, Licorice. He's been scratching for months, has scabs down the center of his back, and I don't know what's the matter."

"Offhand, I can't tell you that either," I said, though the symptoms sounded uncomfortably familiar. "When we're all back in New York, bring him in."

Licorice proved to be a black Domestic Shorthair, a ten-pound neutered male with a large bone structure and a handsome face. He was, I discovered, a very inquisitive and nice cat, but bedeviled for some time by his own desperate need to scratch and bite at himself. In spite of his discomfort, his disposition was friendly, and he purred while I drew my hands over his body.

Scabs ran along his spine, and in some areas his hair was missing.

These signs are good indicators of the little demons I suspected. Fleas are often hard to see on a black cat, but parting his hair to bare narrow paths on his skin, I could see battalions of them racing along his back and abdomen.

"Fleas it is," I said. "He'll need a flea bath, and after that he should wear a flea collar for a while."

"There's something else," said Barbara, "something weird in the litter box. I was pretty sure you'd want a stool sample, so I brought one. Nasty little tiny white things in it."

And I was pretty sure from the tiny white pieces in the stool, very much like grains of rice, as well as the little dried-up bits beneath Licorice's tail, that the trouble was tapeworm. My lab technician confirmed the diagnosis.

The tapeworm was no surprise to me. Fleas can be, and often are, intermediary hosts for tapeworm. The cat had ingested at least one infected flea and developed a new parasite. Those little "rice grains" were segments of the tapeworm he had passed. The adult tapeworm in the intestinal tract can be up to two feet long, and can ultimately interfere with the cat's nutrition and health as well as being a somewhat repellent presence.

So the black cat was in for tapeworming as well as his flea bath. And these things were done.

Licorice, now fine and dandy, became a new friend, and one who only came in for his routine checkup and vaccinations.

Some cats can be loaded with fleas and show no clinical signs. These cats do not have the sensitivity to flea bites that causes the itching and skin lesions. On the other hand, there are truly hypersensitive cats that go nuts under flea attack, and they do sport all the symptoms. They are allergic to flea saliva. You wouldn't think that such minuscule creatures as fleas could actually have saliva, but they do. And some sensitive cats may not have a single flea on them, but nonetheless go through a prolonged period of scratching and licking. It appears that at some time in the past, these cats were bitten by a flea or fleas, and the malady lingers on. This condition can be considered allergic dermatitis, which can only be correctly diagnosed by skin testing. In the course of the test, a small amount of antigen, including flea antigen, is injected under the skin, indicating the cause of the allergy. Sometimes we see an allergic cat with miliary dermatitis—a mass of little pimples on various parts of the body—or patches of licked-bare skin, pink and sore.

It's a case of different strokes for different cat folks: Some cats can have flea infestations and no dermatological problems; others can get one bite and zip!—the allergy acts up every year. My friend Caroline's Queenie starts itching every September and comes in regularly for her flea-antigen shot, and I never see a flea on her sensitive little body.

Fleas are an age-old problem for cats. A condition that I find increasingly common of late is not nearly so old, and yet I see it all over the world.

A few years ago while vacationing in Rome, I bumped into a client of mine, Mrs. Rinaldi, on the Spanish Steps.

"What *wonderful* luck to run into you, Doctor!" she trilled. "My *bella* Vittoria hasn't been herself for days. I haven't used a local veterinarian because we will be in New York very shortly, and because Vittoria finds you so-o-o sympathetic."

Vittoria was the Rinaldis' beautiful Blue-point Siamese, and quite the jet-setter. The Rinaldis split their time between New York and Italy, and Vittoria always traveled with them.

Mrs. Rinaldi invited us to dinner that evening. Jane and I were delighted at the prospect of dining in a Roman home. And while there, I'd have a look at Vittoria.

When I'm away on holiday, I usually bring a small bag along, containing emergency instruments and supplies—a little stethoscope, a thermometer, a few syringes and some important drugs—just in case I run into such a situation. In fact, I started doing this because the need happened so frequently.

That evening, my wife and I entered the Rinaldi living room. Lovely Vittoria was perched on a scarlet pillow, wearing a sparkling narrow diamond collar that she did not customarily wear in New York. Besides the Rinaldis, Mr. and Mrs. Caruso were also there, the latter being Mrs. Rinaldi's sister. The Carusos, from Florence, had been house guests for about two weeks. Both were sipping drinks and puffing away at Italian cigarettes in elegant holders.

After the requisite pleasantries and before a glass of wine, I took Vittoria into a bathroom to examine her. She was as sleek as ever, but her appetite had been poor, her owner said, and she'd been having coughing spells. Her temperature was normal, but her respiration certainly was not. Hmmm. Bronchitis. What kind?

"Where does she sleep?" I asked,

"At night, she sleeps in the guest room," Mrs. Rinaldi replied. "My sister likes having her there."

I made an initial diagnosis of allergic bronchitis and gave Vittoria an injection of prednisone, a steroid, to relieve the bronchial spasms. "Is it possible," I asked Mrs. Rinaldi, "to keep her in an air-conditioned room for a few days?"

"She is not hot?" Mrs. Rinaldi said, surprised.

"No, she is not hot," I said. "Just having trouble breathing. I'd like her to be in a controlled environment—temperature steady, air circulating." I wrote her a prescription for the antibiotic amoxicillin, which could be found at a local pharmacy. This was to take care of any infection that might develop secondary to the bronchitis.

We put Vittoria in the Rinaldis' bedroom, the only air-conditioned room in the apartment. "We're never here in the summer," said my hostess, "and we have the air conditioner only for the occasional very warm day." She set it for moderate room temperature. "But tell me—how could she get bronchitis?"

I told her, and her eyes widened in surprise.

"I think I will say nothing now," she said. "They are leaving in two days."

On the evening of the second day, Mrs. Rinaldi called me. Vittoria, safely away from the source of her problem and breathing clean air, was feeling much more chipper.

I was pleased. But there are several possible causes for allergic bronchitis, and I wanted to be positive about Vittoria.

Mrs. Rinaldi and I arranged for a complete examination in my New York clinic in about ten days.

Back in New York, I gave Vittoria a chest X ray, a blood test, a stool examination for parasites that migrate through the lungs into the trachea, and a tracheal wash. The wash flushes fluid through the trachea, and the fluid is examined for eggs or parasites. Well, she was clean. Vittoria had, as I had thought, a smoke allergy; but it's better to be safe than sorry in case anything was complicating her bronchitis. So Vittoria is a healthy kitty, and Vittoria doesn't smoke any more.

I have known cats to succumb to lung disease almost certainly exacerbated by the smoking habits of their people, and I've known other cats to become asthmatic little coughers and wheezers just like their owners—or their owners' frequent guests.

Secondary smoke is never to be taken lightly.

Mrs. Rinaldi was delighted to have a healthy Vittoria. She told me that she had put up the international sign for No Smoking, a cigarette with a bar though it, in both her American and Italian apartments. Any visiting Carusos would have to go along with it.

"If anything else comes up, may I call you from Rome?" she asked.

"Si, si, Signora!" I replied, in my very best Italian.

My only Italian, in fact.

CHAPTER NINETEEN

Lumps *and* Bumps

R. JOHN SCHIRMER, a renowned plastic surgeon, brought his three-year-old Abyssinian cat into my office for something more than a routine checkup. Since Schirmer's wife had passed away, this cat had become the joy of his life. He called her Sarah, and there was a sweet dignity about her that matched her name. Sarah was a spayed female, a devoted one-person cat. Dr. Schirmer took her with him wherever he went. She accompanied him to his office each morning and tucked herself into a little bed near his desk, perfectly content in these surroundings so long as he was near.

Schirmer's cat was a Ruddy Abyssinian, wearing an orange-and-brown coat with dark brown tipping. She also had a noticeable lump on her flank. I had been recommended to Dr. Schirmer by a colleague at his hospital, and when he came to see me, he was both irate and upset. The story was that two months earlier, he had taken Sarah to her regular veterinarian, who had cared for her since she was a kitten. The visit had been for her first leukemia vaccination. But afterwards Dr. Schirmer had felt a lump where there had been no lump before, and feared it was a tumor or cyst developing at the injection site. He thought that possibly the former veterinarian had used a syringe that wasn't sterile.

And he was in quite a state.

"Dirty needles," he steamed. "Unforgivable. That is exactly where he stuck the needle in. Look at that bump."

Of course he was distressed, because there was definitely something abnormal here, but I didn't think a dirty needle was to blame. That almost never is the case anymore.

After examining Sarah, I told Dr. Schirmer that the lump was indeed a tumor, and of the kind that sometimes occurs following a vaccination. It has nothing to do with unsanitary needles, and fortunately it's fairly rare, but it can happen.

Dr. Schirmer looked skeptical. The most common form of this tumor is a fibrosarcoma, which is a malignant tumor that, after removal, can redevelop but does not metastasize. I thought this was what I was looking at, but I couldn't be positive until I had taken it out. It is widely believed, and I think it's probably true, that the aluminum adjuvant in the vaccine—not a dirty needle—causes this type of tumor. I assured the doctor that it wasn't the fault of Sarah's erstwhile veterinarian. Such a tumor could have occurred no matter who had given the vaccine.

This was, more or less, the good news. The rest of it was that Sarah needed surgery.

Dr. Schirmer urged me to go ahead.

After it was done, we sent the tissue out for biopsy, and it came back positive for fibrosarcoma. Only a minute percentage of vaccinations can cause such tumors, so I like to tell cautious cat owners that if they think of *not* giving standard vaccinations to their cats because of the remote possibility of complications, they should think again. It is wiser to give the necessary vaccines, taking a small chance on a cat developing fibrosarcoma, than to withhold them and have the cat risk death from any of several preventable lethal diseases.

I instructed Dr. Schirmer, when he came to pick her up, to watch the operative site for any signs of recurrence. He assured me emphatically that he would be watching like a hawk and would call me if he noticed anything remarkable.

Sarah, always serene and cooperative, came in many times after surgery for vaccine boosters and minor problems, and everything was fine. There was no recurrence of the tumor. That didn't mean it couldn't happen; but we knew that if it did, we would take care of it.

Sarah's was an intriguing and rather rare case, but I once had an even rarer case, where a single lump affected two individuals.

One was a cat and one was not.

On a nasty day in November, Mrs. Ferguson appeared in my waiting room, taking off her drenched raincoat and croaking a greeting to Joy, the receptionist. She left her long scarf wrapped around her neck and told Joy that she was very, very ill. So was her cat Maggie. Only an emergency for Maggie, she said, would bring her out in a storm, and she'd gotten out of her sickbed to bring the cat in.

"I have a strep throat," she rasped, as I took them both into the examining room. "Maggie's been retching and coughing for the past two days, and her appetite is poor. That's not like her. I'm afraid she's caught the strep throat from me."

That didn't seem too likely, but it was a provocative thought.

Maggie, a little cat of mixed ancestry, was really under the weather. Never mind the retching and coughing; she had severe halitosis, gingivitis and periodontal disease. Her throat was inflamed, and she had, of all things, tonsillitis.

Tonsillitis is something a little different from the usual run of feline ailments. Chances are, it's never occurred to most people that cats *have* tonsils, but they do. Cat tonsillitis, however, is rare, and Maggie was one of the unlucky ones. She was also somewhat unlucky in that no attention had been paid to her mouth for a very long time. But what was more important now was that she had a bacterial infection, causing her left tonsil to be greatly inflamed and enlarged.

I put her on an antibiotic, chloramphenicol, for five days. It comes in a liquid form, and cats don't seem to mind the taste. In fact, some cats like it well enough to lick it off the spoon.

When Maggie and Mrs. Ferguson returned five days later, both were feeling much better but not yet in top form. Nonetheless, Maggie was in good enough condition for us to get on with her dentistry. We put her under for it, as we always do, and under general anesthesia, we were able to examine the throat more carefully. The left tonsil was still abnormally enlarged.

When Mrs. Ferguson came to take her cat home, I gave her some post-dentistry instructions. "Also," I said, "Maggie will have to continue the antibiotic for another five days, and then I'd like to see her."

Mrs. Ferguson, I thought, was still not looking or sounding completely recovered. Something interesting was going on here. The fact is, continuing the antibiotic treatment was less for the benefit of the cat than for Mrs. Ferguson.

"This is not what we call a zoonotic disease," I explained. "But there is an interaction going on here between you and Maggie. Odd as it may seem, a cat's throat can act as a reservoir for a strep infection. It is possible for a cat to get a transient infection from a human who had close contact with it, and show no symptoms of strep, but the strep reservoir could remain active to reinfect a human. In fact, human doctors dealing with recurring strep infections should ask their patients if they have a cat or a dog; and if so, the animal should be taken to the vet for a course of antibiotics to wipe out the reservoir."

"Reservoir," Mrs. Ferguson repeated. "How fascinating."

I thought so myself.

Maggie's next visit showed an improved throat, but the left tonsil remained very enlarged. It might be just a chronically enlarged tonsil, but other possibilities occurred to me as I thought over cases I'd had in the past. It could possibly be a lymphosarcoma, or a squamous cell sarcoma. Both are very serious, and even with proper treatment, their prognoses are guarded at best. But it was no use speculating. I couldn't arrive at a correct diagnosis without a biopsy.

I explained all this to Mrs. Ferguson in great detail. We agreed that as long as we had to give Maggie another general anesthetic for the biopsy, we might as well simply remove the offending tonsil to avoid future problems.

We sent it intact to our pathology lab for a diagnosis.

Seven days later, the lab faxed back a diagnosis of a chronically enlarged, nonmalignant tonsil. It was the best possible scenario! Elated, I phoned Mrs. Ferguson at once to announce the good news.

Very soon, both Maggie and her owner returned to full throat health: Maggie's without a tonsil or any reservoir of infection, and Mrs. Ferguson's without strep.

Meanwhile, I was dealing with a couple who didn't realize that their cat had a lump or bump of any sort. They just knew that Nigel had not been himself for some time.

Henry Noble and his wife, Lydia, owned a gray-and-black Domestic Shorthair either ten or eleven years old. "Ten," said Henry. "No!" Lydia countered adamantly. "He's eleven!" They glared at each other. I began to think the age controversy would blow up into a real crisis in my office. Both parties were really heated up. Over such a little thing!

Fortunately, there were a couple of items the Nobles agreed upon: the cat's name, which was Nigel, and the fact that he was a castrated male.

Henry and Lydia were both science teachers. He taught at a public school for gifted students, and she taught at a small but prestigious girls' school in New York City. With no children of their own to occupy their private hours, they had time to watch over Nigel and dote on him like the extremists they were. You could tell by the way they talked to him that they were truly devoted to their surrogate child. The fact that they came in together was another tipoff. Only in rare cases—like Pawline's first visit, for example—do both 'parents' come in at once.

These two were incredibly proprietary. They both wanted to hold Nigel for the examination, and, of course, squabbled about it. In order not to play favorites, I had my technician of the day come in to hold the cat while I examined him. And both of them loudly described his symptoms at the same time. At last, Henry turned to his wife and said sarcastically:

"Darling, why don't you tell the doctor how Nigel's been acting, and why we are here?"

"That's what I was *trying* to do," Lydia sniffed.

"It seems that Nigel has been losing weight," said Henry, before Lydia could launch into her pitch. "He was a fairly heavy cat, actually quite plump, and now he's looking thin."

"Yes, but he still loves to eat," Lydia jumped in. "In fact, he steals food if it's around."

"He's also drinking more," said Henry. "We never used to see Nigel at the water bowl, but these days I have to fill it twice a day."

"And the kitty litter is always wet."

Okay, fine. Now I thought I knew something. After they'd finished their alternating rendition of Nigel's history, I began the examination.

In examining a cat, I usually start by taking the temperature before the animal gets too excited. Nigel's was normal. Then I took out my stethoscope and examined his heart and lungs. The heart sounds were normal for a cat of ten—or eleven—years of age. I used the otoscope to check his ears, which were normal except for a little excessive wax. With the ophthalmoscope, I examined his eyes, and they, too, were normal. Next, I examined the nasal passages with a special light and a small speculum; also clear. No surprises. Checking the mouth, I asked the Nobles when last Nigel had had his teeth cleaned.

Amazing! Dead silence. Both Nobles shook their heads, mute for once. Evidently cleaning had never occurred to them. But these teeth certainly needed attention.

I shook my own head. I can count on my fingers the number of clients who voluntarily bring in their cats for dental care.

But Nigel's fangs were not the immediate problem. Apparently they didn't interfere with his appetite.

The throat and upper respiratory tract were normal. All joints of locomotion, normal; no arthritis. Anal glands, normal. I went back to the abdomen. Palpating it for a second time and lifting Nigel up off the table for a minute, I could feel how thin and light he was. Obviously, he'd lost a lot of weight.

I next palpated his thyroid gland, which is in the neck area.

Now we had it. The gland was quite enlarged. Again, no surprise. I told the Nobles that the weight loss, increased thirst and enlarged thyroid gland all pointed to hyperthyroidism: overproduction of the thyroid hormone.

"We'll have to take a blood test to confirm the diagnosis," I told them. "At the same time, we'll do a complete blood chemistry and blood count. We also need to get an accurate thyroid level."

They agreed that if the work had to be done, it had to be done.

"Do it," Henry said firmly. Lydia seemed in a mild state of shock and said no more at this point, which was all right with me.

While my technician held the cat, my nurse took a blood sample. Nigel just sat there on the examination table, the very model of an exceptionally good patient. He even purred as his blood was being taken, a contented sound that I suspect was due more to nervousness than any delight in what we were doing to him.

The standard blood test turned out to be normal, but the separate thyroid test showed considerable elevation of the thyroid level. Nigel was, indeed, suffering from hyperthyroidism, and that was the cause of all his symptoms.

On the following day, a Saturday, the Nobles came to the office together. I told them the test results and suggested that we take action quite soon. I didn't think that Nigel was in urgent danger, but there is no knowing how fast the disease might progress in any particular cat. And if we left it unchecked, he would sooner or later die of it.

The Nobles seemed to be taking this in stride. All they wanted, they said, was to have Nigel well again and putting back a little of that lost weight.

As I explained, we had three different avenues of treatment to choose from. The first, surgery, meant removing the enlarged gland. If we did that, it would immediately cut down on the amount of thyroxin being produced in the body. Another option was giving Nigel medication in the form of daily tablets and checking his blood monthly for some time to see if we had achieved the right level of thyroxin. The third avenue would be to treat the cat with radioactive iodine. This might be rather impractical, I noted, because not many medical facilities do this type of treatment and it requires a period of isolation.

They thought for a moment, then both spoke up at once. Lydia won. "We're not good at giving pills to Nigel," she said. "We've tried it many times and failed completely. He seems to have a genius for hiding them and then spitting them up. I think surgery would be the best treatment."

We arranged to do the surgery on Wednesday. Nigel would be released on Friday, and the Nobles would be free to take care of him over the weekend.

On Wednesday morning, the couple brought Nigel in, after having him fast for twelve hours as per my instructions. I thought they'd never stop hugging and kissing him. But all of a sudden Henry tore himself away. "We must go, and we will call," he said decisively. It seemed to me it was something of a dramatic moment for him. I told him that I had his number at school and would call him as soon as the surgery was over. They left quietly.

During the operation, I found one lobe of the thyroid gland greatly enlarged and the other lobe quite normal. Luckily, only the enlarged lobe needed to be removed; the normal-sized lobe would remain, and continue to secrete thyroid hormone at a proper level. We sent the excised lobe to the pathology lab.

It turned out to be a nonmalignant type of glandular enlargement. There was no sign of cancer.

After surgery, I called Henry Noble and told him the good news.

"Operation's over. Nigel is resting comfortably. You can visit him any time from four o'clock on."

Henry was delighted, and asked if he could bring the patient some food. "Not that yours isn't perfectly good, of course . . . "

"Certainly you can. Bring him whatever you like. Or whatever he likes." My clients often ask if they can bring snacks or favorite tidbits to their pets, and I always encourage them. It seems to make everybody happy.

I myself would have been perfectly happy with the snack brought by Henry and Lydia when they arrived to see Nigel at four on the dot, carrying a paper bag emblazoned with the name of New York's fanciest gourmet shop. Cooing with delight at the sight of their recovering loved one, the Nobles unveiled their gifts: freshly poached salmon and smoked turkey. Nigel's favorites.

No wonder he'd gotten so fat before he'd gotten so thin.

When Nigel got a whiff of the salmon, even I found it hard to believe that he had had major surgery only that morning. As Lydia tenderly fed him small pieces of the fish, he purred in real contentment. Nothing nervous about him now.

Nigel came back in ten days for suture removal. He was doing wonderfully well. I had him return in six weeks for another checkup, at which time he was almost completely recovered—free of unpleasant symptoms, thyroid level well within appropriate range and only just the merest tad of convalescence still required.

"We're all back to normal," Henry and Lydia said at more or less the same time."

"I guess so," I thought to myself, as they left the office smiling the same happy smiles—and arguing, arguing, arguing.

CHAPTER TWENTY

Dr. Padwee
Answers
Your Questions

I T WAS A FIELD TRIP FOR THEM and a lot of fun for me—ten curious twelve-year-olds from a local girls' school had brought three adopted kittens in to see me. They all crowded eagerly into my office; the girls, that is, not the kittens.

The visit came about through my new client, Julia Damrosch, their class teacher. She's a schoolteacher at the same school as Lydia Noble. I have about six or seven clients there; one recommends the other, and I can't even remember who was first. Julia's cat, a black-and-white Domestic Shorthair, was about to be mated when we had originally met.

I'd instructed Ms. Damrosch on the mating of her Annabelle as well as on prenatal and postnatal care. Annabelle had given birth to three healthy kittens, which were even more of a delight to their owner than to their mother. Julia, at that time, was giving a course in nutrition to her seventh grade class. It occurred to her that she could use the kittens as living illustrations of how good nutrition fosters healthy cats and also show the correlation between nutrition in people and animals. So when the kittens were seven weeks old and weaned from their mother, she took them to school for an advanced experiment in show and tell—namely, do it and discuss it. She set up a child's playpen in the classroom, arranged so that the kittens couldn't escape through the slats.

The girls took care of the kittens on a rotating basis, and with great success. They learned, hands on, the basics of feeding, cleaning the kitty-litter box, caring for the kittens and maintaining them in good health. On weekends, Julia took them home and played with them herself.

The kitten learning project was in fill swing when Julia brought Annabelle in for a checkup. She told me all about it, and how fascinated the girls were with the experiment. And then she asked if it might be possible to bring the class to my hospital and show her students just how we cared for sick cats and what an animal hospital is all about.

"The girls will have questions, I'm sure," she said. "Would you be willing to have us?"

"Definitely. I'd love it. It's a great idea. Talking to young ladies is right up my alley. I have daughters of my own."

I adjusted my appointment schedule and alerted my staff.

The girls arrived, all bright-eyed with interest.

"The clinic started out as a single brownstone," I told the students. "Then we expanded next door, and now the two houses are a single building." I explained that cats and dogs were usually kept separately, but the intensive care/recovery room held all the patients who needed constant supervision. There was always a technician on overnight duty to keep an eye on them.

We talked about my flowers, the ones in the window boxes facing the street, and I showed them my roses in the backyard garden.

"This is a multipurpose garden," I said. "We can air and exercise the dogs here on nice days, and the staff and I can use it for lunchtime breaks. We also use the garden, sometimes, for sad situations. When we have to put a sick animal to sleep—and that does happen, you know—we let the owners sit here and we bring them tea. They can sit here as long as they like, and when they're ready, they go home."

The girls said, "Awwaahh," and "Aaahhh," and looked concerned.

Enough of the sadness. "But the real work we do here," I went on, "is to make animals well and happy."

We toured the clinic, and I explained the various things that go on in each of our rooms—examination rooms, treatment room, surgery, X-ray department, lab and the cages for keeping our animal patients.

The tour over, I said, "Now, I'm sure that some of you must have questions. But first, I have answers to questions I bet you never thought of. Let's start."

They whipped out their notebooks and looked expectant.

"Is your cat right-handed or left-handed? Observe him as he bats toys or paper balls around the house. Which paw does he use most? If he slaps you or lands a punch on another cat, note the operative paw. But don't be fooled—some are ambidextrous.

"Is your cat territorial? Does she object to guests coming into the house? Or is she a social cat who rubs against guests' legs and wants to be petted? If the friend sits down and puts out a hand, does your cat offer hers? In other words, does your cat have good manners?"

Knowing smiles. Reading from notes, I gave them a few "Did you knows."

"Did you know that cats groom themselves after a meal to remove the buildup of smell from stale food because that might attract a predator?

"Did you know that the domestic cat is the only species of cat that can hold its tail vertically while it walks? All wild cats, including lions and tigers, hold their tails horizontally or walk with them tucked between their legs.

"Did you know that cats can have freckles, just like people?"

At that, a pretty redhead with a sprinkling of freckles on her nose blushed and tittered.

"True," I said. "You can see freckles on orange tabbies. They begin as tiny specks on the lips, gums, eyelids or nose. These specks grow more noticeable as the cat ages. They are called lentigines and are perfectly harmless. We refer to them as a 'normal abnormality.'

"And did you know that cats and people have lived together for more than three thousand five hundred years?

"Did you know that when your cat sheds, it has a lot of hair to do it with? A cat has one hundred thirty thousand hairs *per square inch* on its belly. No, I haven't personally counted!

"Did you know that Mark Twain was a cat lover? He had four cats, and he named them Blatherskit, Beelzebub, Appolinaris and Buffalo Bill.

"Did you know that cats have scent glands? They have them at the base of the tail, on their lips and chin and on both sides of the forehead. When your cat strokes along your legs, it's marking its territory. You didn't know you belonged to your cat, did you?

"Did you know that cats have twenty-four whiskers on the average, neatly arranged in four horizontal rows on either side of the face?

"Did you know that cats' claws grow in layers? So when Mitzi scratches, she's trying to remove the top flaky layers to get to the smooth new claw underneath. When you see what looks like a fingernail trim lying on the rug, that's just what it is.

"Did you know that cats can have bad breath?" I told them about several I have known, and this really made them giggle. And, of course, I added my inevitable little lecture about dental care.

A little girl waved her hand: "I'm Katy. I want to know if cats can have B.O.?"

I had a hard time with that one. "When cats are dirty, they can be very smelly," I began, "but as for body odor all the time, I don't think so. Although there is a curly-coated breed of cat called the Cornish Rex that might have a little trouble with what my kids used to call 'toe jam.' I've heard secondhand stories about a veterinarian having a Cornish Rex patient with a strong odor coming from its toes. He was puzzled, and he asked a person who breeds this kind of cat, and the Cornish Rex breeder said that yes, indeed, Rexes perspire between the toes and need pretty frequent shampoos to control the smell. Now I've never actually sniffed between a Rex's toes, so I can't vouch for kitty B.O. . . . "

Well, that broke them up.

"How about some more questions?"

Eager hands shot up.

A rather spotty young lady asked a question that was clearly close to her own concerns. "Can cats get pimples or acne?"

"Yes, they can. It usually occurs on the chin and sometimes on the face, and generally starts from an area where there are blackheads. The cat scratches and becomes infected."

"Can I give our cat aspirin when he's not feeling well?"

"No! Aspirin is very dangerous for cats. Veterinarians may sometimes give very small doses, but you and your parents should avoid using this drug on a cat. Or any unprescribed medicine."

"We take our cat to the country on weekends. She has a thick coat, but if she stays outside in the freezing cold, can she get frostbitten?"

"Yes, she could. 'Freezing cold'—32 degrees F and below—is just too cold. But a cat's hair does act as weatherproofing. In very hot weather it can insulate your kitty and block out some of the heat."

"My dog had heartworms once. Can my cat get it, too?"

"Certainly not from your dog, and probably not at all. Cats *can* get heartworm, but it's much less common in cats than in dogs. And it's only a danger in hot, humid areas with a large mosquito population, because the tiny little larvae are transmitted by mosquito bite. Prevention: mosquito control."

"My grandmother says that garlic will cure worms in a cat. Is that true?"

"That's an old piece of folk wisdom, but I think garlic—even supposing you can get the cat to eat it—only gives the cat garlic breath and doesn't do any good. We have quite effective worm cures, which I recommend as a better alternative."

"Should I give my cat milk? He's five years old."

"Five? Many adult cats like yours don't want milk any more and don't need it. Just like some grown-up people, they can't tolerate the lactose. Milk causes diarrhea and vomiting in these cats. But if your cat seems to like milk and has no bad reaction, he can have it. And if he does have a reaction and still likes milk, you can try him on a lactose-free milk prepared especially for cats."

"What's a hairball?"

"Well, as you've all observed, cats lick themselves. Then they swallow the hair. It accumulates in the stomach and the intestinal tract, where wads of it either proceed out one end or, more often, get vomited up. These are the famous hairballs. They can look like little golf-balls, though sometimes they come up in the shape of a cigar or a breakfast sausage." (Cries of "Yuck!") "But if you keep your cat groomed, brushing away excess hair, you'll keep the hairballs to a minimum."

"Is it all right to kiss a kitty on the nose, or can you catch something that way?"

"It's fine if it's an indoor cat, a kitty you know, certainly your own cat. But for cats that go outdoors a lot, you just don't know where they've been and what they've put their little noses into. So you have to be a bit careful. Kiss clean kitties only!"

"Our cat gets fleas all the time. Should we get an electronic collar for her?"

"No, electronic collars don't work well at all, and I wouldn't advise you to spend your money on one. A flea shampoo bath is a much better idea, but be sure to keep your cat warm until she's completely dry."

"Do cats really love fish, like they do in stories?"

"Yes, most cats really love it. They don't *need* fish, because they're not natural fish hunters, but they do take to it and it's good protein. Not that they should eat *only* fish. They shouldn't; they need a more balanced diet. In fact, cats can get seriously addicted to fish, especially tuna, and it's sometimes hard to get them weaned away from it."

"Is it normal for a cat to eat grass?"

"It is, but cats don't have a dietary need for it, and they can't digest much raw vegetable matter. I think they just like chewing on it. And it may do some good: Sometimes it actually irritates the stomach just enough to make the cat throw up its latest hairball and clean out its system. On the other hand, sometimes if a cat is ill, he might have what we call a depraved appetite, in which case he might eat an excessive amount of grass and vomit a whole lot more. If this happens, it's time for the vet."

"Our cat is great at catching mice. Once I found three dead mice at the top of the cellar stairs. How many mice can a cat catch in a day?"

"That depends on the availability of mice and how much the cat is being fed. But I've known cats to catch as many as ten mice in a day. And though we humans don't like the idea, they do tease captured mice. You've heard of the cat-and-mouse game? The cat catches a mouse, lets it get away, captures it again, and often goes through this sequence many times until the mouse gives up. What the cat is doing here results from a combination of natural instincts, which have nothing to do with malice toward mice. The so-called game is a combination of the cats' hunting instincts and ability, their playfulness, and their wish to show their owners what they can achieve. That's why your cat left those mice where you'd be sure to find them. This is a universal cat game, and it's played in city apartments, country houses, city shops, country stores, warehouses and barns and even in big department stores. Wherever cats meet mice—and this is just about everywhere—this game is played. It's not really a game, though, is it? A game needs two sides willing to play. In this case, only the cat, not the mouse, is having fun."

"Can my cat get Lyme disease, like from ticks?"

"Yes, it can, but it's not nearly as common in cats as in dogs. There's no vaccination, so the best preventive is to keep your kitty out of tall grass whenever you can. And pick off any ticks the instant you see them."

"Our cat is very fat. Can we put him on a diet?"

"First, you take him to a veterinarian to find out if his obesity is caused by overeating or some sort of illness. If it's just too much food, the vet will give you a diet for him. If he's sick, the vet will treat him."

"How do cats squeeze themselves into very small spaces, like drainpipes and behind things?"

"It's the magic of their bodies. They have tiny collarbones, literally vestigial clavicles, that don't get them stuck in narrow places. They also have very loose coats that allow them to squiggle through openings that we wouldn't even have thought *were* openings. When you get a chance—try it on any kitty—put your hand down on a cat's coat and move it back and forth. The coat will move with your hand; it's as loose as that. And that's why a cat can squeeze through the most unlikely places."

"Our cat always seems to throw up on my mother's favorite carpet. She drives my mother nuts. Why does she do that?"

"Well, it's her favorite carpet, too. She feels secure there. She gets a better footing on carpet than she does on a bare floor. She wants a little traction when she's heaving!"

"Does a cat have as many teeth as humans do?"

"Not quite. An adult cat has thirty teeth."

"If something happens to the mommy cat after kittens are born, should you find another mother cat to nurse them, or can you bottle-feed them?"

"It's much better to have them nursed if you possibly can. The milk that comes out for the first few days after the birth is called colostrum.

This early milk is very high in antibodies, giving the newborn kitties protection against many diseases. So having them nursed is far preferable to anything else. But if that isn't possible, you can buy replacement milk for your orphans from your veterinarian or from pet supply shops. These commercial feline formulas, such as Havolac and Veta-Lac, can be given with an eyedropper until the kittens can lap up the milk themselves—usually at about two weeks. At six weeks, you can start giving them small quantities of mashed-up real food."

"Our cat is sixteen years old and acts like a kitten, leaping on chairs and chasing toys. How old is he in human terms?"

I liked this one. "He's pretty lively for an eighty-year-old," I said. "Sixteen years in a cat is equivalent to eighty in a human. Of course, these age calculations are only approximations, but I'll give you a little chart so you can evaluate a cat's 'human' age. Write this down:

"At six months, ten years. Eight months, thirteen years. Twelve months, fifteen years. Two years, twenty-four years. Four years, thirty-two years. Eight years, forty-eight years. Ten years, fifty-six years. Twelve years, sixty-four years. Fourteen years, seventy-two years. Sixteen years, eighty years. Eighteen years, eighty-eight years. Twenty years, ninety-six years. Twenty-one years, one hundred years! Maybe twenty-one-year-old kitties should get a telegram from the President, just like hundred-year-old humans do! Of course, as I said, what I've given you is only an approximation. Other charts may vary equivalent ages, but I think these numbers are about as close as we can get."

I sneaked a look at my watch. I thought the visit was instructive and fun, and the students seemed to want to hear more. But I did have patients to see, and surgery to do.

Their teacher said: "I think we really have to go now. It's been wonderfully informative, but we can't take up any more of the doctor's time."

As they left, Katy and two of her friends asked a final question: "How can we get to be veterinarians?"

"You'll be a vet if you want to," I said. "Half of the students in veterinary school today are women. But you'll have to work at it. Because you know something else? It is easier to get into law school now than it is to get into a veterinary college. But you must remember this: What you'll be doing is—a far, far better thing! I wish you good luck."

Postscript: Teacher Julia Damrosch was pretty efficient. Not only did she make a potentially dull subject like nutrition fascinating for her students, she also interested them in the veterinary profession *and* found homes among them for the growing kittens.

CHAPTER TWENTY-ONE

Cats-22

I

T WAS ONE OF THOSE WINTRY SUNDAYS in the middle of December. I knew the next day might be snowy when I saw the late afternoon sky and felt the moist air on my face. To me, it felt and looked and smelled like snow. The television weatherman confirmed it on the late night news: There was going to be a big one—at least by New York standards, where the merest flake makes strong men cry and traffic grind to a halt.

Most days I drove into Manhattan to work, and whatever the weather, I would be driving tomorrow. There was no doubt in my mind that the entire local transportation system would be fouled up, from suburban trains to city subways and buses, and I had a strong urge to have my own hands on my own wheel and my car in the garage nearest me. It was a fifty-mile drive from my house to the clinic, so I set my alarm clock for five A.M. instead of the customary six to make sure I would get there on time.

It was already snowing heavily by the time I left, and the radio was telling me how many inches would be landing here, there and up in Poughkeepsie. This was not just a major snowfall; this was almost a blizzard. Driving and listening, windshield wipers clacking away, I thought, "Probably I'm doing this for nothing. Probably all my appointments will be canceled, and I'll be sitting there alone talking to the animals."

To my surprise, after I'd left my car at the garage and arrived at the clinic at a quarter past eight, there were already three people in the waiting room. One was a young woman sculptor named Mollie Rose who lived in SoHo, an area of artists' lofts and galleries just south of Greenwich Village. She had a Siamese cat who was at that moment having a vociferous conversation with her. I cut in to talk about the weather, and she said she'd had to leave her house early in order to get here on time, and luckily she had found a taxi immediately in spite of the streets being almost completely deserted. She hadn't wanted to miss giving Rembrandt his leukemia vaccine, which was due that day. More than most cat owners, she was particularly conscientious about this, because years ago her cat Picasso had died of leukemia, and she couldn't bear to lose another to something that could so easily be avoided.

Rembrandt the cat picked up his conversation where he had left off, and I went to change into my white coat to start the day.

I took care of Rembrandt and my other two patients while the doorbell and the telephone kept ringing. It was really amazing, I thought. It was the kind of day that you wouldn't expect people to show up. The streets were deserted, and there was a sense of all sounds being muffled and nothing happening, as if we were all in a white cocoon. But my staff showed up, people did come, and the phones did ring, and we were as busy as on a normal day and maybe even more so.

I was taking a culture from a cat's throat when my receptionist told me Mrs. Simpson wanted to talk to me on the phone. It was very important, not exactly an emergency, but extremely urgent. Mrs. Simpson was one of my really major clients.

"Yes, Mrs. Simpson."

Mrs. Simpson is to be remembered as the lady with the twenty-two cats. Every winter she and her husband and kids would go to

Florida by train and get compartments for all—that is, all people and all cats. The Simpsons were very wealthy: It was their custom to reserve several compartments for the cats, which would travel uncaged all the way in their own little rooms. Appropriate arrangements were made for feeding, watering, kitty cleanup and possibly television, for all I know.

One time when they had to leave the cats at home, they hired someone to look after them and gave the cat-sitter carte blanche at the butcher shop. The cat-care person fed them ground filet mignon, in effect the very finest hamburger, every day, at huge cost—hundreds of dollars for the time the Simpsons were away. I suppose it was still cheaper than hiring a train, but it wasn't what I'd call a very well-rounded menu. For their part, the Simpsons decided that they'd rather have the cats with them.

Now, on this snowbound day, Mrs. Simpson had a problem. She and her husband Henry and their six kids and twenty-two cats were supposed to be leaving for Florida first thing the next morning, and she had suddenly remembered that her cats hadn't had their annual feline leukemia virus booster shots. We had sent her a reminder the month before, but what with planning the trip and everything it involved she had completely forgotten about the vaccinations until this moment.

What to do? The booster shots were overdue, and she was afraid to travel without having the cats vaccinated. Mr. Simpson was at his Wall Street office, her household help hadn't made it through the storm, and she couldn't see bundling twenty-two cats into a taxicab single-handed, even supposing she could find one. Oh, there was a doorman, and she could hire a limousine, but-but-but . . . Well, of course there were veterinarians in Palm Beach, and there had been one she used to see once in a while, but unfortunately, he had retired. She knew of absolutely no one she could trust to vaccinate her cats.

Clearly this song and dance was going someplace, but that place was probably not my clinic.

"And I can't postpone the trip," she said despairingly. "All the children are home on school vacation, and I've made reservations on the train for sixteen compartments—"

Sixteen! My mind reeled. How many compartments are there to a railroad car, anyway? And how many people would be willing to share space with a carload of cats?

"—that's twenty-two cats, two to a compartment, so, eleven; six children, two to a compartment, one for Henry and me, and one for the two maids, and I just can't cancel."

No butler? Surely the cats must have a butler, I thought.

But, be that as it may, there seemed to be no way to solve this puzzle except to tell Mrs. Simpson that I would make a house call some time before nightfall.

She was relieved and grateful, but somehow she didn't sound particularly surprised. We had both known all along that there was no other way.

Luckily, by four o'clock, the crush had eased up at the clinic, and I was able to leave the rest of my appointments to my associate, Dr. Jody Norton. By that time of day, taxis were in full spate on the avenues but had become impossible to get, so I decided to take the car out of the garage. I would need it, anyway, for driving home.

It was still snowing, less heavily now, and the streets were a mess of churned-up slush that would be icing up after dusk. Somewhere, blocks away, I could hear a snowplow at work, but the streets near the clinic were a minefield of snow dunes and ruts and cars grinding their wheels and buses honking their horns.

I had to get uptown to Park Avenue and Eightieth Street and then head for home. It looked pretty bad, but I didn't think I'd have any trouble. I was used to driving in sleet and snow. My experience as a young country vet making farm calls in the middle of the night on dirt roads in all kinds of weather had prepared me for virtually anything nature could ask of me. I had new snow tires on all four wheels, and I was ready for anything.

Almost anything. I had miscalculated a little. The snow-clogged

skies made the winter day shorter than usual, and nightfall was already coming down around my ears when I emerged from the garage
and headed uptown through a maze of honking cabs. I was right about
not having any trouble, but I was wrong about being able to get uptown in anything like my usual time. With all the skids and impreca-
tions of the other drivers and some frozen traffic lights, it took me
over an hour to do a ride that usually takes twenty minutes.

And it was cold when I got out of the car. Little icy needles stung my
face and darted under my scarf. I wanted to dash back to the warmth
of the car, but instead, I grabbed my black bag and went into the apartment house, where the doorman said he would watch my car for me.
It was now a little after five.

Mrs. Simpson, elegantly coiffed and dressed as always, greeted me
with more than usual enthusiasm. She took my coat and hat, put her
arms around me and gave me a startlingly warm hug and kiss. "You've
saved all our lives!" she gushed, handing my damp outer wear to one
of two maids I saw hovering about. Apparently they had managed to
show up after all.

We sat in front of the fire drinking hot tea and nibbling cinnamon
toast, while discussing the logistics of the trip the next day. Melted
snowflakes dripped off my beard and down my neck as the logs crack-
led. Sunny Florida seemed like a wonderful idea to me at that point,
though packing twenty-two cats did not.

Come to think of it, where were they?

Not in front of the fireplace, which was a bit strange.

"My, my," said Mrs. Simpson. "Florrie and Louie and Chloe were
right here on the hearth until the doorbell rang and you came in. Do
you think they know something's up?"

"Probably," I said glumly. "They usually know as soon as their people start packing."

I looked around at comfortable sofas, all unoccupied, and open
doors and endless hallways. The cats, all twenty-two of them, seemed
to have fanned out in this huge apartment and disappeared.

"Well, let's give it a whirl," I said, pocketing a supply of prepared syringes.

She led me first to her son Billy's room, and somewhere down the hall out of my sight, I heard the scrabbling sound of a cat digging into floorboards for traction and taking instant flight.

"That would be Archie," Mrs. Simpson said placidly. "As you probably remember, he's quite highly strung."

I didn't remember. Basically all I remembered about these cats was their arrival in my consulting room two by two, carrier by carrier, passively but heavily resisting all attempts to get them out on the table. They failed, of course, but they all acted pretty much alike—trapped, paralytic and resentful until I started chatting to them, at which point they perked up and purred. But I never learned all their twenty-two names nor remembered which was which.

A boy working on a model airplane looked up from his desk as we tapped and entered.

"Billy, this is—"

"Hi," we said together.

My spirits rose. Four cats were lying very peacefully on Billy's bed, somnolent and all cuddled up together while Billy fitted airplane parts. I wondered if he'd given them a little sniff of his glue, but I thought it best not to ask.

Mrs. Simpson held each cat in turn, while I vaccinated with the hair-thin needle designed to slide right under the skin. This is an absolutely painless procedure, and nobody squawked to warn the others that something was going on.

In moments, it was done.

Four down and eighteen to go, I thought. So far, so good.

Easier than I expected. Onward to the other eighteen.

Now, of course, we couldn't find them. Not a single one. Archie must have spread the word.

"We're just going to have to do this very methodically and very quietly," said Mrs. Simpson in hushed tones, leading me to her son

Harold's room. She tapped and opened the door. Harold let us in, and as he did so, a long, lean shape flashed past his feet and fled down the hall.

"Sorry," he said cheerfully, "but I have three others—whoops! Two! Come in quick!"

He closed the door behind us, and I observed, without great pleasure, one cat scuttling under the bed and another leaping to the top of a wardrobe.

But there were three of us, and we had the two cats trapped. In a minute or two, the dual deed was done.

Sixteen to go.

It was at this point that the truly hard and totally ridiculous part began. A quick but quiet sweep of all the rooms in the house turned up absolutely nothing. I've known individual cats to hide for anything from minutes to hours, but I've never known sixteen cats to melt into the woodwork and stay there without a sound. Usually when you go around calling, you'll hear a tiny little meow from somewhere in the house, and then Pow! you've got him. But this apartment was too big, and there were too many hiding places.

Mrs. Simpson called up the reserves.

"Harold! Billy! Lauren! Claire! Ellie! Carolyn!" Doors opened and children popped out, looking helpful. "Gracie! Celeste!" The two maids appeared, neat in black and white.

The lady organized her troops. Four adults and six children of various sizes and spirits scurried around searching energetically for cats. Once again, doors opened and shut, and people popped in and out, the maids intense and the children laughing a lot and bashing into each other. This is like something out of a Feydeau farce, I thought. Or the Pink Panther, with me stumbling around, unpantherlike, as Chief Inspector Clouseau, to the sounds of scrambling feet and cries of "Tootsie, get over here . . . Honey, get out of the piano! . . . Charlie, come down from that shelf!"

For a little stretch of time, there were intermittent whoops of

"Gotcha!" I rushed to do my stuff, syringes at the ready, soothing words upon my lips, until—at twelve down and ten to go—there was a lull. We searched tops of bookcases, under beds, behind half-open doors, inside drawers, in kitchen cabinets and laundry baskets, playing what seemed like an endless game of Now You See Them, Now You Don't. As for me, this hide-and-seek thing was not exactly part of my job description, nor quite the tranquil atmosphere I like to engender for my work. I must say I started to hang back a little when I saw Mrs. S. bump her head against the post of a huge double bed, and her hair went oddly askew. I realized then that she was wearing a wig, and I felt a little bad that I had observed this and went to wait near the fireplace.

Mr. Simpson came home from Wall Street into the living room with snow in his hair and a bewildered look. He sat in front of the fire and didn't say a word, just shook his head once in a while as loud cries and faint meows wafted down the hall.

Young Billy stuck his head in at the doorway. "C'mon, Doc! We gotta bunch!"

I scurried after him. Five children, a mother and two maids wearing pained expressions each had a cat pinned to the mat. I attended to them briskly. Okay, that's another eight. Surely this must be the lot. But no! Raghead and Madonna are still missing. The hunt commenced once more. I must say I was about ready to throw in the towel when one of the children suggested looking in the guest room, which had been closed all day for the sole purpose of keeping cats out. So, of course, there they were, snuggled on a pillow in the guest room closet. Also in the room were eleven large cat carriers, all lined up for the next day's trip, a ton of cat food—a kind they don't sell in Florida—and a tasteful selection of matching food bowls.

Two quick shots, and I was done. One final conference regarding eating arrangements for the trip: two bowls of water per compartment, and feed the cats only at night. Dry chow would be best. Would they be wanting tranquilizers for the trip? "No, but I think I'll need one," Mrs. Simpson said faintly.

I made my farewells to the entire household and went out into the drifting snow. It went right straight down my neck. For a moment I thought a month in Florida sounded ideal, and then I thought: not with twenty-two cats. It was not much past seven o'clock. I ploughed home under a clear night sky.

The next day, driving in again, I thought about the whole experience of trundling uptown in a socked-in city to vaccinate twenty-two cats. I must have been addled, I thought. So many things could have happened in that dreadful traffic. And what if we hadn't found all the cats? I shuddered. Mrs. Simpson would never have let me leave. And yet, catching the cats hadn't been all that bad. The whole thing could have been a much worse experience and taken a lot longer. At least it was over and done.

The city was a blanket of snow, and the cleanup noises were pleasantly muted. I thought of the multiple Simpsons settling into their multiple train compartments, and I didn't envy them a bit.

A few days later, just as I was getting ready to leave the clinic, my receptionist handed me the phone. She had a tiny little smile on her face. "It's Mrs. Simpson," she said.

I gritted my teeth. What was it *now?*

"Yes, Mrs. Simpson?" I said guardedly.

She was all apologies. So sorry to disturb me again, but in the rush she had forgotten to take along the cats' vitamins. Could I possibly send some?

Of course I could. I was so relieved that there was no major problem, I would have sent her anything. The fact is that few cats need vitamin supplements, and Mrs. Simpson's healthy brood was not among them. But easing Mrs. Simpson's mind would do no possible harm to her robust legions, and even though I'm pretty sure you can get cat vitamins in Florida, I immediately started wrapping up a supply to ship to her via UPS.

"And have a wonderful holiday," I said. "All thirty-two of you. Please."

CHAPTER TWENTY-TWO

The Long
Goodbye

JOSHUA HAD BEEN ONE LUCKY KITTY CAT. He'd lived a long and happy life with Bill and Carolyn Egmont and their two children, who'd grown up with him. I'd known him almost as long as I'd known Pawline, and during that time he had been a remarkably healthy and trouble-free cat. But now beloved Joshua was a venerable eighteen years of age, and as the years caught up with him, the orange-and-white Shorthair was inevitably slowing down.

In fact, Josh was indisputably a geriatric patient, and these cats have to be watched very closely. A lot of little things in the system begin to wear out and break down. I consider all my cats geriatric after the age of fourteen, and it's a good thing they don't know they're considered elderly, because some of them act like kittens for a long time after that. The average lifespan today for a well-cared-for cat is fifteen to sixteen years, so Joshua had already beaten the odds. Some cats live into their twenties, but not really very many of them.

When I got the call, I hadn't seen Joshua for some time.

One Saturday night, Ellen and Joe Newcombe, friends of the

Egmonts, came to dinner and played with Joshua as they usually did. "He's just like a kitten," said Ellen. "As quick and playful as he ever was."

But the Egmonts knew better. Joshua was behaving in ways they hadn't noticed when he was seventeen. He didn't play for very long periods of time, and he tired easily. He drank much more water, and after a burst of activity, he had a little cough. These are changes you would be aware of only if you saw a cat every day and knew his normal habits and rhythms. For a few minutes at a time, he was his younger self; and then he wasn't. Even though he looked and often played like an energetic youngster, Carolyn could see the difference.

And she knew that I would want to see him.

But she kept putting off a visit to my office. After all, he *was* getting older. "Aren't we *all* slowing down a little?" she reasoned. "And isn't he entitled to some peace at his age? All that jabbing and poking at him!"

His appetite had started getting a little erratic. He was drinking even more water than usual. And then one day when Joshua was at his water bowl, Carolyn saw him drinking truly excessively. He drank and drank and then he began to vomit. That was excessive, too. When the vomiting finally stopped, he seemed quite weak, not at all the gingery cat of before.

Carolyn wondered if the episode had been caused by the treat she'd given him, some lobster she'd brought home from a restaurant she and Bill had gone to the night before. Whatever the cause, she knew it was time to bring Joshua into my office.

I diagnosed a case of acute gastritis, most likely from the lobster. "I'll give him a gastric sedative, and keep all food and water away from him for twenty-four hours," I told Carolyn. "After that he should be fine. For now."

While petting the cat and checking him at the same time, I said to Carolyn, "It's been some time since I've seen Joshua. He needs his geriatric checkup."

She looked a little shamefaced. "I know. I've been meaning to bring Josh in for some time, but I guess I just let it slide. So long as we're here, let's do it now."

I put him on the scale—weighing is a ritual part of our general examinations—and noted that he'd lost a pound and a half since his last checkup over a year before. Going over his history with me, she told me that Joshua's appetite was not what it used to be. Once a cat who would eat anything that wasn't nailed down, he had become a picky eater. That was why she had given him the lobster as a treat. It was one of his favorite foods, and she had hoped that it might stimulate his appetite. Also, he was much thirstier than in the past, and over this last year, urination had become more copious and more frequent.

The examination included a complete blood count, a urinalysis and a blood chemistry. This would give me an "attitude": a picture of the different systems of the body, including kidney functions—which were my particular concern. We also took a chest X ray to check any abnormalities in the lungs, the bronchi or the heart; and to further assess the heart, we did an electrocardiogram. Joshua's teeth, for too long neglected, were covered with tartar, and his gums were inflamed by severe gingivitis. I didn't want to address this problem for the moment; I'd rather wait until all the lab reports were in to get a reading of his general condition.

Next day, the lab reports and X-ray results came in. After assessing these tests and the EKG, I arrived at a diagnosis: chronic kidney and heart disease, as well as the dental disease already observed. The kidney diagnosis, based on Joshua's symptoms as well as the lab reports, was chronic interstitial nephritis. This meant that the kidney tissue showed degeneration; and the kidneys, which normally act as filters, could no longer filter efficiently.

"He's getting to be a really old fellow," I said to Carolyn, "and much as I dislike suggesting it, you might think about—"

"I don't want to think about it," Carolyn said. "I want him well. As well as possible, for as long as possible."

I put Joshua on an antibiotic and prescribed a special diet for the kidney disease.

"Special diet?" Carolyn murmured dubiously.

Owners are often wary of special diets. The very idea sounds a little daunting.

"This is no problem at all," I said. "No trouble to give to a cat. The servings are already fully prepared."

Several different companies put out this special diet, and most veterinarians carry the food on their premises. I always keep it on hand. It is a diet low in phosphorus, high in nitrogen, low in protein, high in nonprotein calories—namely carbohydrates—rounded out with B vitamins and taurine.

I made sure Carolyn understood that this was not a cure, but a means to maintaining the kidney function for as long as Josh could hold out. The heart disease—cardiac enlargement, for which I prescribed digoxin—compounded Joshua's problems, but we would ease them all as best we could.

We also wanted to clean his teeth. Dental diseases have an effect on the heart: Bacteria in diseased gums get into the bloodstream and travel to the heart, which in Joshua's case was already in trouble. Clean teeth would also make eating more comfortable, but I did not want to risk giving him anesthesia at this time. We'd try doing dental work without an anesthetic. One good thing: no extractions were needed. Even so, it wouldn't be easy to get the whole mouth done. Joshua was an amiable cat, but no one could expect him to stay still for more than a few teeth at a time. This meant that his owners would have to bring him in for short visits twice a week for about seven weeks. Luckily, the Egmonts lived not far from my office, so the frequent trips weren't too much of a nuisance.

Joshua was a patient patient. He just sat there on the table as we scaled two or three teeth at a time, letting us do our quota until his dental problem was corrected. The antibiotic given for the kidney condition also helped to arrest the gingivitis, and he was a much more contented kitty with his mouth cleaned up.

With his new diet, plus the medication, Joshua clearly felt a little better. He even looked better, for a while. But after six months or so, his condition began to deteriorate. And slowly it worsened. He developed congestive heart failure, and became weaker because of the reduced cardiac output. He could still get around the house, but with his heart and kidney diseases, as well as his advanced age and tiring legs, he moved very slowly.

He was the Old Man of the family, and that is what the Egmonts called their dear Josh. Carolyn and Bill and their children loved him deeply and became more and more distressed as they watched him weaken. There were days when he did not even attempt to climb into the litter box, but instead urinated on the floor beside it. He was, despite many small meals, getting thinner and smaller; his eyesight was failing, and he would often walk into doorjambs and chair legs. The Egmonts could not bear to see him suffer. They watched him try to crawl into his basket, the one by the radiator, and he couldn't manage to get in. This was it! No more of this for Josh! Together they decided that euthanasia would be the correct, and kindest, path to take.

Of course I want my animal patients to lead active and happy lives, but I am aware that in the end they must, like all living creatures, depart this earth. But, as I told the Egmonts, we can grant them a wonderful privilege that is denied to us. We can let them go in peace; we can touch and hold our beloved companions as the veterinarian ensures them a swift and painless death.

The whole Egmont family came to the office with Joshua. It was difficult for me to be completely detached, but I was pleased that the Old Man had very good veins in his front legs. Giving an injection would be easy. Carolyn held him in her arms, and Bill and the children gently laid their hands on him. Joshua gave a few little sighing purrs.

I took an alcohol swab and wet the fur down; I held the vein with my left hand and had the syringe in my right. It was a syringe with a very fine needle, the kind used for human babies.

Joshua never felt the needle going in. He never moved, never quivered. I'd given him an overdose of an intravenous anesthetic. It took only three seconds and he was gone, all that was left of him lying limp in Carolyn's arms.

Afterwards, we went out into the rose garden.

There were tears, of course. We arranged to have Joshua cremated, with the ashes, in a small canister, sent to the family.

Joshua really was a lucky fellow . . . an old guy with a full life, and a peaceful end surrounded by those he loved most.

And now we come to Pawline, cat of all cats: Pawline, whose perils and hairbreadth escapes—most often from the clothes dryer—had kept her owners and me aghast, exasperated and amused over the years. Pawline had joyfully used up her nine lives, and then some. But at over eighteen, she was a very old lady indeed. Not the oldest cat I have ever known, but ripe with years.

Tough little barn cat that she was, Pawline met old age with dignity. Because of the Gardners' love for her, she was even more fortunate than Joshua. Her decline into terminal age was gradual and comfortable. Nancy brought her in for geriatric care according to schedule and called me periodically to keep me posted. She told me that she preferred to keep Pawline at home to the end; preferred to let Pawline determine the time. The Gardners, five of them now, were making arrangements for her send-off. They were practical people, they knew the time was short, and they had a friend doing a little woodworking for them.

Pawline spent more and more time on the Gardners' king-sized bed. Where once she had loved leaping up and romping around, she now found solace in sleeping much of the day. The bedroom was her favorite place to be. When Nancy came home and Pawline wasn't at the door to greet her, she knew she'd find her on the bed.

And one day, that was where Nancy found her. Standing in the bedroom doorway on a fine spring afternoon, she looked over at the bed and knew at once that Pawline was no more. She had gone to sleep and would not wake again.

It is sometimes said that sick cats crawl away to die. I think they don't; I think they just go someplace and can't get back. Pawline wasn't sick. She had lived her life allotment, and she had simply gotten up onto her special place for one last time.

The Gardners' carpenter friend Bill had already made and burnished a little wooden casket just big enough to hold the kitty. Nancy lined it with Pawline's worn, much loved and much washed cotton blanket. John nestled her gently into its folds. Seventeen-year-old Claire, just that little bit younger than Pawline but still scarcely more than a child, said a few choked-up words to her silent form about how sweet she had been when Claire, as a toddler, had pulled her tail and yanked her around and hugged her relentlessly without ever eliciting a meow of complaint, and what a good friend she had been ever since. Lucy and Robbie, eleven and ten respectively, each laid a favorite toy beside her, with young Robbie having the honor of placing her choicest toy, a chewed and drooled-upon felt mouse, near her front paws. John closed the little casket and nailed it shut. Nancy phoned the news to Pawline's many friends.

The family immediately drove to their country house, near where Pawline had been born, to bury her in the backyard. The children dug the grave, and John fashioned a cross of two wooden sticks. When it was firm enough to hold for a very long time, he painted it with Pawline's name and the dates of her birth and demise.

The next afternoon, friends and neighbors who had loved the Gardners' kitty came to the house to say goodbye. Some had driven more than sixty miles in order to be there. John lowered the little box into the grave. Nancy spoke of the long-ago camping trip when Pawline had come into their lives and how clueless they had been about caring for her. How, in a sense, Pawline was their first child, or at least the first little being they had loved as family, and how the human children had had Pawline's company every day of their lives.

John covered the grave. Each member of the family threw in a handful of sod. Then he tamped down the earth and positioned the cross bearing Pawline's name. Thump! with a mallet, and it was firmly in place.

Robbie and Lucy had written a poem with a little editorial help from Claire. Lucy pushed Robbie forward to the graveside. In a clear voice, stumbling only a little over some of the longer words, he bade farewell to Pawline for all of them:

Pawline dear . . .
Many fulfilling long-lived years
Yet you were brave and had no fears
Many things you have seen and done
Many adventures that you've been on

Pawline you've been our pride and Joy
You've lived longer than us girls and boy
And yet you've still kept young at heart
Sadly now from us you part

You brightened our hearts and been our closest friend
And we are ever sorry that it all had to end
Though down here you've spent your lives of nine
We hope you have many more in Heaven divine

Now that all's been said and done
We know you have more adventures still to come
We wish you well, Pawline dear
And from angels' dryers please stay clear.

There was a little throat-clearing, and then the farewell party began.

Nancy called me several weeks later and thanked me, as she had before, for the care and interest I had shown Pawline and her family. She told me that the phone was constantly ringing with callers eager to give her a new kitten. Funny, how many available kittens had suddenly appeared!

"I'm sure there'll be plenty more where they came from," she said, "but I'm not ready. I'll just have to wait a little longer to decide."

There was a short pause, and then she added: "But somehow, I do think that eventually you'll be seeing me with a tiny new patient. Maybe soon."

And she was right. It wasn't long before I did.

Index

Domestic or American Shorthair breed, 44-46, 56
"double-pawed" (polydactyl) cats, 163-64
Dristan, 154
dry coat, 115

ear mites (*Otodectes cynotis*), 174-77
  as commonest cause of ear disorders, 174
  and hematoma, 176-77
  unsanitary conditions and, 12
electrical shock, as emergency, 110
electrocardiogram, 229
Eliot, T. S., 159-60
emergency situations, "Ten Commandments" of, 110
  falls from height, 110, 131-32, 137-39
  malnutrition, 182-83
  and non-emergencies, 115-16
  swallowing foreign substance, 110, 111-112, 118-19, 123, 124, 125-30, 157
entropion, congenital, 50
euthanasia, 210, 231-32
exercise for overweight cats, 107, 120
eyes and eye problems
  congenital, 50, 162, 165-66
  conjunctivitis, 13, 16
  diet and, 181-85
  retinal degeneration, 182
  seeing in the dark, 180

fading kitten syndrome, 93-94
fall, as emergency, 110, 131-32
  from upper story, 110, 137-39
feline immunodeficiency virus (FIV), 41, 149
feline leukemia virus (FeLV), 38-41, 149
  vaccination against, 17, 40, 220
feline urologic syndrome (FUS), 101-3, 107
fibrosarcoma, vaccination and, 200-201
fish, as food for cats, 188, 214. *See also* diet and nutrition
FIV. *See* feline immunodeficiency virus
fleas, 12, 18
  as carriers of disease, 144
  cats allergic to, 188-91, 194-96
  and defleaing one's home, 192-93
  electronic collars and, 213
  flea-antigen shots, 195, 196
  as hosts for tapeworm, 195
freckles, cats with, 211
fur mites, 148

FUS. *See* feline urologic syndrome

gastritis, 228
gastroenteritis, 73
genetic mutations, 24, 160, 161-62
gingivitis, 152-53, 201, 229, 231. *See also* dental problems
grass, 168, 214
Greer, Milan, 53-54, 162-63
grooming
  necessity for, 49, 52, 213
  self-grooming by cat, 210, 213

hair
  amount of on cat, 211
  long-haired cats, 49, 51, 52
  as weatherproofing, 212
  See also grooming
hairballs, 115, 168, 213, 214
"hairless" cats, 51, 171
halitosis, 152, 154, 156-57, 201, 211
Havana Brown breed, 44, 52-53
hearing and hearing problems
  and ataxia (loss of balance), 173
  and cats' adjustment to hearing loss, 174
  cats' hearing range, 175, 177-78
  ear mites and, 173-77
  and "silent meow," 178
  in white, blue-eyed cats, 24, 162
heart problems
  congestive cardiomyopathy, 94
  dental diseases and, 230
  heartworm, 212
  nutrition and, 182-83
  in old cat, 230, 231
heat, cats' liking for, 46-47
heat period (estrus), 60-63
hematoma (of ear), 106, 176-77
high-rise syndrome, 138-39
Himalayan breed, 44, 52
hit by car, as emergency, 110
HIV virus, 149
hyperthyroidism, 205-7

incontinence, 103
infections
  antibiotics used for, 153-54, 177
  and cystitis, 100
  ear mites as source of, 174-77
  dangers of, in boarding cats, 15-16, 17